Brainard Cheney and

The Search for a Hero

Brainard Cheney and
The Search for a Hero

A Literary Biography of a Southern Novelist,
Reporter, and Polemicist

James Edwin Young II, Ph.D.

MMJW BookHouse

2016

Published in 2016 by MMJW BookHouse
P.O. Box 111, Eastman, Georgia 31023

For more information on this book and the author:
http://www.lightwood.com

The Lightwood History Collection: Book 10

ISBN: 978-0-9864060-1-0 (Hardcover)
LCCN: 2016917456

Portions of this work originally appeared in 1979 as a PhD dissertation at Vanderbilt Peabody College under the title: *The Search for a Hero*

To

My wife, Vera Kondratieff Young

and my four sons:

James Scott Young
Clyde Benjamin Young
Yuri Kondratieff Young
Sevolod Kondratieff Young

THE LIGHTWOOD HISTORY COLLECTION

Book 1: *The Lightwood Chronicles: Murder and Greed in the Piney Woods of South Georgia, 1869-1923, being the true story of Brainard Cheney's novel,* Lightwood compiled by Stephen Whigham

Book 2: *Lightwood* by Brainard Cheney

Book 3: *River Rogue* by Brainard Cheney

Book 4: *This is Adam* by Brainard Cheney

Book 5: *Devil's Elbow* by Brainard Cheney

Book 6: *They Don't Make People Like They Used To* by Addie Garrison Briggs

Book 7: *Rivers, Rogues, and Timbermen in the Novels of Brainard Cheney* by Michael R. Williams, Jr.

Book 8: *When Theo Met Meta: A History of the Coleman-Shaw Families of Valdosta, Georgia* by Daniel Shaw Coleman

Book 9: *Letters from Sister: The Correspondence of Wylena Hargrove Davis and Dorothy Hargrove Stoeger* by Wylena Hargrove Davis and Dorothy Hargrove Stoeger

Book 10: *Brainard Cheney and The Search for A Hero* by James Edwin Young II, Ph.D.

Acknowledgments

The author would like to thank the following special collections departments for the use of photographs and unpublished letters and documents: The Special Collections and University Archives of the Jean and Alexandra Heard Library of Vanderbilt University; Princeton University's Department of Rare Books and Special Collections; the Department of Special Collections of Western Kentucky University; The Hargrett Rare Book and Manuscript Library of the University of Georgia; Nancy Bray Davis at The Ina Dillard Russell Library of Georgia College and State University; and the Smyrna Public Library (Smyrna, Tennessee).

Special thanks for the use of personal photographs to Mary Williams of Nashville and the late Ida Read of Murfreesboro, Tennessee.

I would like to offer a special thanks to Stephen Whigham, historian and publisher for MMJW BookHouse, whose interest in the life and writings of Brainard Cheney made this publication possible.

Contents

Preface
Conversations with Brainard Cheney

I first came to know the Southern novelist Brainard Cheney and his wife, Frances Neel Cheney, in the fall of 1975. I was a student at Peabody College of Vanderbilt University in Nashville, Tennessee, working on a Ph.D. in English. While taking a course in bibliography and literary research from Edwin Gleaves, the director of the Peabody Library, Dr. Gleaves stopped me after class one day and asked if I lived in Smyrna, Tennessee. I answered that I did. Smyrna is a small town 25 miles southeast of Nashville from which I commuted each day in an old rickety 1965 Volkswagen camper. Dr. Gleaves asked me if I would be interested in occasionally giving Mrs. Cheney, his head reference librarian, a ride into Nashville. She also lived in Smyrna and did not drive.

I was happy to have someone from Peabody accompany me on my commutes to Nashville. Mrs. Cheney was a delightful companion. Over the next year, during our commute, we had many conversations about the history of Nashville, Peabody College, the future of education, and Southern Literature. One afternoon, as we drove back to Smyrna from Nashville, she mentioned that no one had studied and assessed her husband's contribution to Southern Literature. I knew that Brainard Cheney had written several influential novels about Georgia, but I did not know that in 1972 Vanderbilt University had purchased, for a substantial amount of money, all of his personal and literary papers. The collection included manuscripts of his published and unpublished novels, short stories, plays, political and literary articles, and letters to book publishing editors, journalists, and politicians. The "Cheney Papers" also included over 2,000 letters of correspondence with some of the South's leading men and women of letters, including detailed correspondence with Robert Penn Warren, Flannery O'Connor, Allen Tate, Caroline Gordon, Andrew Lytle and many of Vanderbilt's Fugitive and Agrarian members.

I thought, what a treasure of unexplored primary documents. I accepted her invitation and thus began an academic journey that took me two years to complete. The result was *The Search for a Hero*, a study of the life and writings of Brainard

Cheney, which was accepted as a Ph.D. thesis at Peabody College in 1979. During those two years of study, I read all of the documents in the Cheney Papers in the Special Collections and University Archives of the Jean and Alexander Heard Library at Vanderbilt. I conducted over fifteen hours of personal interviews with Brainard Cheney at his home, Idler's Retreat, in Smyrna, Tennessee.

Cheney's wife, who was a grandniece of the Confederate "boy-hero," Sam Davis, inherited Idler's Retreat in 1946. It was an impressive, two-storied, brick antebellum house, situated on eight acres of land, among towering maple and black gum trees. For the Cheneys, the house served as a meeting place for the area's intellectual and artistic community. Students from Peabody College–where Mrs. Cheney taught library science for thirty years–faculty and administrators from that college and Vanderbilt University, and the Cheneys' many literary friends from all over the South were entertained in that gracious home. Grace Zibart, a literary friend of the Cheney's and owner of Zibart's bookstore in Nashville, said Idler's Retreat was "as close to Gertrude Stein's 1920s as we're likely to have anywhere in this part of the country."

Idler's Retreat, the home of Frances and Brainard Cheney, located in Smyrna, Tennessee. *(Courtesy Mary Williams)*

As I worked, month after month, in Vanderbilt's Special Collections Department, reading all the manuscripts and letters, I began to see a pattern of development in his life and writings. Born June 3, 1900, Cheney was raised in the Wiregrass and pinewood region of Southern Georgia as a member of a prominent family who owned over 1000 acres of timberland. His father, Brainard Bartwell Cheney, Sr., had served in the Civil War, read law in Dublin, Georgia, and become a land speculator and lawyer in the region. Unfortunately, Cheney's father died before Cheney was eight years old, and his death left a paternal vacuum in Cheney's life. The pattern that I began to see from his papers, novels, and our interviews was that due to the early death of his father, Cheney struggled all of his life to find a model and ideal to guide his behavior and give meaning and significance to his life.

Brainard Cheney in his study at Idler's Retreat, circa 1970s. *(Courtesy Mary Williams)*

In *The Search for a Hero*, I trace Cheney's religious, political, and artistic development as he searched for an ideology that could sustain and nourish his life. I begin with Cheney's youth, describing his early life, education, and relationships with the land and people of rural South Georgia. Later as a young man in the 1920s, Cheney turned his back on his cultural heritage. Swayed by the radical thought of that period, he became, politically, a liberal; religiously, an agnostic; and socially, an emancipated man, free of Victorian morals. He left Georgia and went to Nashville, studying for a time at Vanderbilt. There he came to know and form friendships with Allen Tate, Robert Penn Warren, Donald Davidson, Stanley Johnson, Andrew Lytle, and several other members of the Fugitive and Agrarian groups.

Caroline Gordon, author and professor, and her husband, Allen Tate, were close friends with the Cheneys. She acted as a literary mentor to Cheney in his early attempts at fiction. Examining their exchange of letters, I began to see how an established writer could help a beginner. Robert Penn Warren also assisted Cheney. Over the years of their friendship, Warren read and offered suggestions on most of Cheney's fiction, and Cheney often returned the favor. He helped Warren substantially with a crucial scene in *All the King's Men* where Willie Stark makes his first effective political speech.

For thirty years, Cheney earned his living as a newspaper reporter for the *Nashville Banner* and as a political aide and speechwriter for Tennessee's Senator Tom Stewart and Governor Frank Clement. As a cub reporter on the *Banner* Cheney enjoyed the friendship of Ralph McGill, who later became executive editor of the *Atlanta Constitution*. Their reporting days reveal what life was like during the "roaring twenties" in Nashville. Later as a Capitol Hill reporter and as a political aide, Cheney's dreams of an ideal society collapsed. Witnessing the corruption and meanness of political life in Tennessee and in Washington D.C., his political views changed from an optimistic liberalism to a tough-minded conservatism.

Following the lead and persuasion of Allen Tate and Caroline Gordon, Cheney, along with Frances, converted to Catholicism in 1953. After his conversion, his thinking became deeply religious, and he attempted in political essays to form a synthesis between religion and politics, a synthesis he called Christian Political Realism. Cheney's fiction also was affected by his conversion, especially by the belief in the possibility of humanity's redemption. In his unpublished novels, *The Image and the Cry* and *Quest of the Pelican*, he allowed his religious ideology to eclipse the organic fabric of his story. Yet in his four published novels, *Lightwood* (1939), *River Rogue* (1942), *This is Adam* (1958), and *Devil's Elbow* (1969), he achieved a successful blending of religious ethos and plot. These four novels were set in Georgia and cover a period from 1874 to 1945, with a cast of characters ranging from frontier backwoodsmen to contemporary Georgians.

Cheney not only recreated characters and events that have long faded from the Georgian scene, but also he wrote of a larger human subject—humanity's proper relationship to life. Each of his protagonists was a person of remarkable heroic stature, who because of his arrogance or pride or selfishness, was ultimately found insufficient to meet the challenges of life. The hero's downfall paved the way for a new relationship with life, one based not on pride and power, but on an acceptance and acquiescence to a Higher Will.

The Search for a Hero begins with an examination of Cheney's youth in rural Georgia, describing his early life as a boy born into a moderately wealthy family with deep Southern traditions, and continues with an analysis of his relationship with his father and mother and Robin Bess, a distinguished mulatto overseer of their farmlands, who, after Cheney's father died, became a paternal figure to the fatherless boy. Cheney's third novel, *This Is Adam*, draws on this personal relationship with Robin Bess and the history of the Altamaha River basin area of Dodge and Telfair counties in Southern Georgia. The character of Adam, based on Robin Bess, also serves a pivotal role in Cheney's final published novel, *Devil's Elbow*.

The following pages introduce the works of Brainard Cheney as both a novelist and essayist, placing him among the significant writers and contributors to the intellectual and artistic work of mid-twentieth century Southern literature.

CHAPTER I
Early Life in Rural Georgia

To understand Brainard Cheney as a man and a writer, we must begin at the beginning—in the history of his boyhood. What were the days of his childhood and youth like in southern Georgia? What types of traditions and codes of conduct shaped him? What were his parents like, and how did they treat him? What were his conceptions of himself, and how did he react to the expectations put upon him by those whom he loved? From these primary relationships and from this setting sprang the ideas, issues, questions, and conflicts that Cheney struggled with throughout his life and tried to express in his writings.

Brainard Bartwell Cheney, Jr. was born June 3, 1900, in Fitzgerald, Georgia, son of Brainard Bartwell and Mattie (Mood) Cheney. Cheney's father had moved to Fitzgerald in

1888 and made his living as a lawyer and part-time farmer. He was a strong, rough, industrious man whose ancestry went back one hundred years into Georgia history. By contrast, Cheney's mother was a refined Charleston lady. Her father had been a respected medical doctor in Charleston, and she had grown up in the genteel Southern tradition. Cheney wondered how his father was able to persuade her to leave the security of Charleston for what she was later to call the "wild frontier" of rural Georgia.

Cheney's memory of his father was vague and sketchy. He remembered a few dramatic incidents, but for the most part, he retained only a general impression of what his father was like:

> He was a man six feet tall, and in that respect, I bear no resemblance to him. He had white hair and a large grey beard and mustache; at least it was grey by the time I knew him. He was relatively remote to me—the youngest child. He had six children—three died from diseases in infancy and were buried before we moved to Lumber City.
>
> I came along late in his life, and I suppose he. . .well, I never supposed much about him. He was a sort of God-like old man with a beard to me. He never touched me. My mother performed all the discipline. He would sometimes say, 'That boy ought to be 'cow-hided.' But he never laid a finger on me. I soon learned that there was

nothing behind his talk; a child is very intuitive about those things. . .He died when I was eight.

I can't remember many experiences with my father. We lived in a large old house with gross gables and surrounded by porches. It had a hall running through it from front to back, which was characteristic of houses in that part of the country. In the back hall, which was sectioned off by a curtain, my mother had placed a cot for him to rest on during the day. One afternoon, I remember lying down next to him as he slept. After a while, he began sleeping heavier and heavier; then suddenly that grey-bearded mouth dropped open and let out a sound that scared the hell out of me. I got up and ran into the yard where the sun was and slowly recovered from his snoring. (Cheney, Interview 5 Nov.)

While researching his family's history for material for his novel *This is Adam*, Cheney discovered more about his father. He had been born on a plantation in 1845, near the fork of the Oconee and Ocmulgee rivers. "His father, Richard R. Cheney [Cheney's grandfather], having inherited a thousand acres and slaves, having married somewhat more, was comfortably 'fixed' as the saying is. . . .The war—which is variously called the Civil War, the War Between the States and the War for Southern Independence, depending on what part of the country you come from—broke out when he was a boy of fifteen, and before it was over, he was in it" (Cheney, "To Edwin Jessup"). [Note: Edwin Jessup, of Eastman, Georgia, was Cheney's brother-in-law and a timber business associate in the 1920s.]

Toward the end of the war, with most of the older officers having been killed, Cheney's father was made captain of a small company. Rumor had it that he was one of the youngest captains in the Southern army. He was a bright and capable young man with a prodigious amount of energy.

At the end of the war, the South had been conquered and its economy ruined. There was no money in the country except for "Confederate money, which they used for wallpaper. So 'Big Bud' [Cheney's father] not only plowed, but he rafted timber and ran a crossroads store. He eventually read law in a judge's office in Dublin [Georgia] and began to practice law" (Cheney, "To Edwin Jessup").

For several years, Cheney's father prospered as a lawyer of honesty, integrity, and energy. As his wealth increased, he moved his family in 1905 to Lumber City, Georgia, where he began buying and selling large tracts of land:

> He, in conjunction with two partners, had planned to
> open up sand mines, a sawmill, kaolin and terra cotta
> clay works on land that he owned. But the partner with

the money went broke in another venture, and the rail-
road which was to have been built through their property changed its route and went another way. And after a
life of unremitting hard work . . . and in the face of these
setbacks, he died in his sixtieth year [1908], leaving a
widow and three small children. (Cheney, "To Edwin
Jessup")

One can only guess at the impression this great hulk of a
man left on a small boy of eight. His father must have seemed
like a heroic, mythical patriarch—possessing remarkable qualities of will, endurance, and energy, romantically appearing to
tame a wilderness with strength and imagination. Cheney
mostly recalled the bigness and mystery of this giant figure and
the vacant space left in the family at his death.

In contrast to his father, Cheney's image of himself as a boy
was filled with self-disparagement. He said that he was small
and sickly, hardly speaking until he was four years old. He was
slow and awkward. His peers usually chose him last in the
games at school. He did, however, swim well, and that was a
great consolation to him. He did average to poor in schoolwork
because he could not keep his mind on the daily lessons. He
often seemed to be in a world of his own. "I remember once
being so involved in a story I was silently telling myself that I

jumped in my desk and shouted out. Of course, the teacher didn't know what to think, and I felt like a fool" (Cheney, Interview 5 Nov.).

He often felt as if he had somehow failed his father. "Whenever I would meet any of the men from town, they would always look down at me and say, 'This is Brainard's boy?' and I would feel so damn small. I didn't have a very high opinion of myself as his son" (Cheney, Interview 5 Nov.).

Besides trying to walk in the steps of this giant, there was also the heavy burden of fulfilling his father's dream of restoring the family's wealth and position to a pre-Civil War status. And finally, there was the moral stricture of his father's last words. "Always try to do what is right: it is the only thing that counts when you come to die" (Cheney, "To Edwin Jessup").

Cheney's dream, however, was not that of his father. Farming was not for him, and the land (2,100 acres) was more of a burden than a blessing. By the time of his twenty-fifth birthday, he managed, through a series of mishandlings or lack of interest, to rid himself of the land and to escape the clutches of rural Georgia (Cheney, Interview 12 Dec.).

After his father's death in 1908, his mother, Mattie Cheney, was left alone to take care of the family. She was poorly prepared for such a task. She had been shielded from all the business problems, a typical custom in those days, and found herself in the position of not even knowing how to write a check, much less provide for her family.

She was intelligent, educated, and strong willed; she quickly learned how to survive on her own. The family had money coming in from a store they leased in Fitzgerald; they received a little produce from the small tenant farms on their land; and near their house, they had a fine garden and fruit trees:

> We had in our back yard, right out from the kitchen, a smokehouse, and beyond that was one of the best Scuppernong grape arbors in South Georgia. I swear they were wonderful. It must have covered an acre. One of the staples of our pantry was grape jelly, grape preserves, and grape wine. It didn't take much money to live on in those days. We had a garden, beyond the mulberry and chinaberry trees at the end of the yard, where we raised corn, sweet potatoes, tomatoes, and other vegetables. We also kept some chickens and cows. . . .So we managed to provide most of our own food. (Cheney, Interview 12 Dec.)

Cheney's mother was a great influence on his life. She was a pious and devout Christian who often read to him from the

Bible and from *Pilgrim's Progress*. She encouraged him to improve himself and to make his mark on the world, and she was not above laying down the law to him about his misconduct and physically enforcing it:

> She never spared the rod with me. I grew up in the days of corporal punishment, and I got plenty of it. First with the back of a hairbrush and then when I got to be a good big boy, she whipped me with a riding whip. She had been a horsewoman in her earlier days in Charleston. (Cheney, Interview 5 Nov.)

It was difficult to be both a father and a mother. The absence of a paternal figure probably moved Mattie to a sternness and strictness that was beyond her natural feelings. "I didn't learn till after my mother's death. . . . She told my sister that she loved me best. But she never gave me that impression. I never heard it from her lips" (Cheney, Interview 5 Nov.).

Aside from his mother, Robin Bess was the most significant influence in Cheney's early life. Robin was a highly-regarded mixed-race man, the son of a white slave owner and an African American slave, who farmed about one hundred acres of the Cheneys' land. He also oversaw several smaller tenant farms for them. Cheney's father had defended him in a trial when Robin was young, and Robin had stayed with the father afterward as his foreman. Through the years, Robin became one of the elder Cheney's most trusted friends.

When Cheney's father died, Robin stayed on to help the family as best he could. In Cheney's adolescence, Robin was the man whom he looked up to. He respected him and learned from him. Robin became, in effect, an adopted father. This was, certainly, a rare occurrence in the history of Southern literature—a Southern writer learning about life and about how to be a man from an African-American tenant farmer.

Years later in 1953, at Robin's funeral, Cheney read a moving testimonial to this man whom he had loved. It was later expanded into an article and printed in the town's paper.

I remember him then, invariably overall-clad and wearing the broad-brimmed black wool hat of countrymen of that day. His skin was a ginger brown, his features Negroid, his forehead high, and his eyes, a luminous brown of a fine intelligence. He wore a scraggly graying mustache, and when he lifted his hat, he revealed straight graying hair. He walked erectly, without any stiffness—indeed, I am sure, without any consciousness of his bearing. He was quiet and, in a gruff way, gentle. He stuttered, yet it never in any way detracted from his dignity.

I have never heard a responsible white man make a derogatory statement about him. My opportunity to know what the members of his own race thought of him has been more limited, but the evidence I have had indicates great respect—he was usually chosen by them to head up their money-raising enterprises for church and community. He was loyal to the race with whom fate had cast his lot, and they believed in him. . .He was not only trusted and respected by those of his own race, he was universally admired by white people far and wide.

He took me fishing and hunting as a boy. I have slept in his yard and in his house. . .but he never allowed me to violate my "place," any more than he thought of violating his.

Later, I logged and rafted timber with him, camped out with him, listened to his inimitable story-telling. I suppose Robin never had a chance at any sort of schooling. At all events, he could neither read nor write. Moreover, he stuttered. Yet, despite this handicap and his ignorance of the literacy artifices, he was one of the few great story tellers that I have ever known ("Of the Old South").

Here was a man who filled the paternal vacuum in Cheney's life. Here was a man who was not an amorphous, mythic, and inaccessible figure, as his father had been. Robin was a man of flesh and bones, of integrity and humanity, and a man who was always there for Cheney.

In time, the relationship between Robin and myself came to transcend the conventions of the old system, but we never failed to observe the surfaces. We said the same sort of things to each other that we had always said, but we knew that we meant more by them. I enjoyed a grand, silent intimacy with him for twenty-five years. We were united by some profound experiences, which we rarely referred to and when we did, only obliquely, or by some common place which covered its reality. ("Of the Old South")

Cheney says that it was always understood between them that he would tell Robin's story. It is sad that Robin did not live to see the publication of *This is Adam* (1958). It was dedicated "to the memory of ROBIN BESS (whose character and works inspired this story)."

However, Robin's son, George Bess, who used to write Robin's letters to Cheney, did read the novel. He said:

"The book is wonderful. There are a million things that I want to say and could say about it, but none of them would neither add nor diminish the fact that the book is just wonderful. I am grateful—I sincerely appreciate your attitude, and would like to thank you sincerely for your contribution to the memory of my father." (Bess)

From these beginnings and personal relationships, we can start to see the forces, powers, and issues that Cheney would spend a lifetime struggling with and trying to articulate. His father had left him with a deep sense of inferiority that would take him a decade to overcome. His obligations to the past, to the land, and to his father's dream would haunt him for years, becoming a force that he would eventually have to overthrow.

He continued to respect the moral courage and fortitude of his mother, although he would later flamboyantly reject the religion that she had taught him, professing himself to be an "Agnostic Materialist." He wanted to find his own answers to the basic questions of existence: questions about God, human nature, and the meaning of life.

From Robin Bess, he learned many things. He developed a keen insight, like Robin's, into the character of men and their social relations, a love of the tall tale and folklore of Georgia, and a unique understanding of the problems of the Southern African American people. Listening to Robin's stories of his own difficult past, Cheney developed a sense of history that later affected the way he viewed the events of his life and the events of the South. He began to see the way individual lives take part in larger movements, and how the past affects the present and future.

Cheney had ambivalent feelings about leaving his homeland. He wanted to be free of Georgia, yet he loved it. He was determined to overcome the limitations of his youth and to participate in the larger world outside Lumber City. Yet he sensed that even though he would someday leave, he would never be entirely free from the problems, forces, and conflicts of those early, formative years in the rural South.

CHAPTER II
Student and Reporter

When Cheney graduated from the small, rural high school in Lumber City in 1916, his desire to leave Georgia and make his way in the world was only an undefined restlessness. It was to take him seven years to break finally with the land and the traditions of his youth. Before he could decide his first step in this adventure, world events came crowding into his life. In April of 1917, nearly two years after the sinking of the Lusitania, and after a resumption and increase of unrestricted submarine warfare, President Woodrow Wilson declared war on Germany. This was to be "the war to end all wars," the war to free mankind from tyranny and "to make the world safe for democracy."

Several of Cheney's friends rushed to the induction centers, but he was undecided. He felt the innocence and confusion of his youth and was determined to wait until he could clearly see what he wanted to do. He was in no great rush to join in a war effort that he felt unprepared for and scarcely understood, yet he supposed that in a few months he, too, must volunteer.

His mother, who had guided most of his life up to that point, saw his hesitation and confusion. Fearing that he was unprepared for such a venture, she shrewdly suggested that he attend The Citadel in Charleston, South Carolina, for a couple of years to further his education and to prepare him for military service. This seemed right to Cheney, so in the fall of 1917, he enrolled as a cadet in one of the South's oldest military academies.

Cheney hated military life. The rules, regulations, and codes of conduct went against the casual, individualistic quality of his youth. He was a Huck Finn in a military straitjacket. The world of the Academy seemed old and inhospitable with none of the warmth and grace of his early Southern life. He constantly received demerits for misconduct in "dress, manner, and bearing." His fierce individualism, lack of attentiveness, and physical clumsiness could not be molded into the military pattern of alert uniformity. He spent nearly all of his free time and weekends marching off demerits in the school's detention square. (Cheney, Interview 5 Nov.)

Cadets marching on parade grounds of The Citadel, Charleston, South Carolina.

Many years later, he wrote to a fraternity brother, contrasting the life that he enjoyed at Vanderbilt to those early days at The Citadel:

> My pleasant recollection of fraternity life is. . . when for the first time I lived in a fraternity house. A shy, red-headed and unfavored country boy, who had found the military discipline of The Citadel cold and harsh and had finally revolted against it, I warmed and came out of my shell under the open-hearted camaraderie of those older brothers. (Cheney, "To Harry Rider")

After two years of military life, Cheney received his corporal chevrons from The Citadel—a symbol that although he was a reluctant soldier, the college saw some hope for him. When the United States signed the Armistice of November 11, 1918, ending World War I, many of the young cadets stayed on at The Citadel. Cheney, however, declared his "separate peace" with military life, and in the spring of 1919, he unreluctantly left The Citadel.

For the next five years, he alternated between working and furthering his studies. The two years at The Citadel laid down the foundations for his education, yet he realized how little he knew and how much was left to be learned. He continued his formal education with one semester at Vanderbilt in 1920 and a summer term at the University of Georgia in 1924. But most of his learning came from self-education, through an exchange of ideas with the people he met, deliberate reflections about life, and a program of broad and abundant reading. During these years, he tried his hand at a number of different types of work. From 1919-20, he worked as a bank clerk in Lavonia, Georgia; from 1920-21, he operated his own crosstie and timber camp back in his hometown; and from 1921-24, he taught school and later was made principal of several small, country schools in rural Georgia.

During these years (1919-24), he read widely and became astonished, impressed, and later converted to many of the new ideas that were disturbing and influencing America in the first two decades of the twentieth century.

There had always been books in his mother's house, and he had read Thackeray, Dickens, Scott, and Irving as a boy. His mother had often read to him from the works of Shakespeare and Dante, the *Bible*, and *The Pilgrim's Progress* (Cheney, Interview 12 Dec.). Now, after work in the evenings, he continued his reading. He read more of the classics of literature, branching out to Balzac, Hugo, Flaubert, and Dostoevsky.

But it was not the classics of literature that stirred him the most. It was the new political and religious thinkers who were causing a revolution within him. In search of answers to his questions about God, human nature, and society, he read T. H. Huxley (*Ethics and Evolution*), Max Eastman (*The Masses* and *The Liberator*), Robert Ingersoll (*Why I Am An Agnostic*), George Bernard Shaw (*Unsocial Socialist*), and Karl Marx (*Das Kapital*) (Cheney, Interview 18 Jan.). He started to see the world in a totally different way from that of his early training. He began to see the world through the eyes of those new, radical thinkers. He started to think of himself as one of the new "emancipated" men—emancipated from religious mores, from traditional ways of thinking, and from the stifling influence of the past. Scientists, philosophers, and political thinkers were saying that the great mysteries of the universe were ultimately knowable by man, that nature followed scientific laws, and that society could be made better and more equitable through good will and reason. Utopia, Heaven on earth, in this century, was achievable. Religion was superstition and not to be countenanced by the emancipated mind. Religious morality was the opiate of the people promulgated by the wealthy and the clergy. Anything and everything was possible in a world freed from the shackles of the Victorian past.

In the foreword to his autobiography, the historian, Will Durant, wrote of a similar transition in his own life. He spoke of a "profound transformation which modern science and research have brought in the faith of the western world. . ." producing changes that "have unsettled the mind and morals of many generations of uprooting the customs and beliefs in which those generations grew" (Durant). Later in the book, Durant recalls a moving talk with the socialist Henry Alden that convinced him that he was not alone in his struggle:

So you thought, when you gave up the old faith, that you were quite alone? But you were just one of the millions and millions. The whole world is undergoing the same change that has nearly broken you. Copernicus began it, Voltaire carried it on, and Darwin completed it; it is the main line of the thought of Europe in the last three hundred years. No mature mind in the western world can ever believe in the old theology again . . .

The idea of a better world on earth will for large classes of people take the place of the hope in heaven, and we shall have great waves of Utopian aspiration. I think it will be a wonderful age, a renaissance not only of the intellect, but of all the powers of man (Durant).

Cheney, like Durant and many others of their generation, became, politically, a liberal; economically, a socialist; religiously, an agnostic; morally, an emancipated man; and socially, a Shavian scoffer at Victorian and bourgeois manners. It is ironic that he would later spend a large part of his middle and late years repudiating these positions that so strongly gripped his young mind.

In 1924, Cheney left Georgia for good. During the past seven years of transition, he had overcome many of "the limitations of his youth." He was now more experienced, more confident, and better read; he had tasted some of the world and was ready for more; he had filled in many of the gaps in his education; and he was excited about the new ideas in science, politics, and religion.

In the fall of that year, he again enrolled at Vanderbilt University to deepen his knowledge and to take part in its intellectual community. Vanderbilt in the 1920s was the closest thing to an Ivy League school that the South produced. It was half-mockingly, half-seriously called "the Harvard of the South." Its tradition was one of Classical Humanism, an approach to learning freed from religious bias and steeped in the classics of Greece and Rome. It was one of the last schools in the nation to drop the requirement for language competency in Latin and Greek.

Vanderbilt had a few elements within its faculty and student body that were modern and progressive. The Fugitive group of poets and critics had flourished a few years earlier (1915-22), producing an influential journal of their poetry, and there were several economists on the faculty who believed in the new socialistic ideas in America.

In 1956, members of the Fugitive group met for a reunion at Vanderbilt University. Brainard Cheney stood proudly, pictured on the top back row, with his fellow literary friends from more than thirty years previous.

The Fugitives celebrate a reunion in 1956 at Vanderbilt. First Row (seated): Robert Penn Warren, Dorothy Bethurum (Loomis), Merrill Moore, John Crowe Ransom, Sidney M. Hirsch, Donald Davidson, Louise Cowan, William Yandell Elliott. Second Row: William Thorp, Andrew Nelson Lytle, Jesse Ely Wills, Alfred Starr, Louis D. Rubin, Jr. Third Row: Allen Tate, Cleanth Brooks, William C. Cobb, Rob Roy Purdy, Richmond Croom Beatty, Frank L. Owsley, Randall Stewart, Brainard Cheney, Robert Jacobs, Alec Brock Stevenson. (*Courtesy Vanderbilt University Special Collections*).

Cheney found the work at Vanderbilt difficult but stimulating. He took courses under Edwin Mims, the chairman of the English Department, and Walter Clyde Curry, the celebrated Chaucerian scholar. Outside of class, he met members of the Fugitive group (Donald Davidson, Merrill Moore, and Andrew Lytle), beginning friendships with them that would last for years. He was not to meet Robert Penn Warren, Allen Tate, and

Caroline Gordon until five years later, and of all the Fugitives, they were to have the most dramatic effect on his thinking and writing.

Cheney had two good semesters at Vanderbilt that year. He studied diligently, earned good grades, and made lasting friendships. Unfortunately, he had to hold down a part-time job at a banking company during the year to meet expenses, and at the end of the year, he realized that the job was not going to be enough to get him through college. On top of his financial worries came the traumatic news that his mother had died in June of 1925. He took it very hard. She had been close to him for a long time, guiding him, and from time to time quietly reassuring him. When he had proudly professed to her that he was agnostic, she had simply responded that religion was not a subject to be argued, that one believed by faith. She told him that because he had always been a serious person, he would someday return to God.

After her funeral, he went back to Nashville, confused and weakened. He began drinking heavily, his resistance to disease went down, and he caught a cold that was complicated by an infection of his kidneys. He was forced to spend several weeks in bed recuperating. When he returned to his job, he learned that he had been fired for missing too much work. In the fall of 1925, he pulled himself together and decided to leave school and to look for full-time employment. A fraternity brother, who had been a part-time reporter, helped him get a job on the *Nashville Banner*. This began a new chapter in the education of Brainard Cheney (Cheney, Interview 25 Jan.).

Cheney was ready for a change from the purely academic life. Because he wanted to know more about how people lived beyond the university walls, he jumped at the chance to become a reporter, even though the pay was only $17.50 a week.

He was able to keep an apartment on Vanderbilt's West Side Row because the University had more space than it needed. It was that year that he took on a new roommate who was also a reporter on the *Nashville Banner*—the famous Ralph McGill. McGill was a great influence on Cheney. He was a colorful, erratic, yet intelligent and generous man who was later to become the editor of the *Atlanta Constitution* and recipient of a Pulitzer Prize for editorial reporting. In the 1950s and 60s, McGill was often thought of as "the Conscience of the South"; he was one of the few Southern newspaper men who supported the Supreme Court ruling on desegregation and the civil rights movement of the sixties.

Ralph McGill, Vanderbilt graduate and later celebrated editor of the Atlanta Constitution. He and Brainard Cheney were roommates and fellow newspapermen for the Nashville Banner during the 1920s.

In those early years, McGill was the H. L. Mencken of the South. He was well read and had a phenomenal memory— quoting names, places, and long lines of poetry at the drop of a hat. He was quixotic, flamboyant, and sometimes impish. He had been kicked out of Vanderbilt in 1922 for writing a column in the *Vanderbilt Hustler* accusing the administration of embezzling money. In addition, he had participated in an outrageous social prank. His rival fraternity had sent out special engraved invitations to one of its formal dinner dances at the Hermitage Hotel. Only Vanderbilt's most socially acceptable were asked to come. This offended McGill's sense of democracy. He stole the plates from which the invitations had been printed, ran off about one hundred extra copies, and distributed them to his friends on campus. To make the party truly an affair of the people, he magnanimously extended invitations to Nashville's derelicts, bootleggers, and "madams" (Martin).

McGill, who was several years older than Cheney and already established on the *Banner*, took Cheney under his wing. Together, they explored the then wild world of Nashville, from the high society of Belle Meade to the speakeasies of Printers' Alley. Cheney fondly remembers their friendship:

> Looking back on that bright distance it seems to me that its glamour for us came of the romance of journalism, the then new notion of Bohemianism and simply our youth. Perhaps I should mention, too, the corn liquor that we drank—indeed, the whole Prohibition predicament! But the ebullient and prodigious spirit of that time, and for me its inspiration, was McGill himself.
>
> In those days of my apprenticeship, I had every reason to be quiet and modest about my talents. But I burgeoned under his warmth and camaraderie, for he gave

himself to the cub and the copy boy even as he did his peers. ("Notes on Ralph. McGill")

In his biography, *Ralph McGill: Reporter*, Harold Martin gives an account of a story that Cheney and McGill did together:

> McGill and Cheney often collaborated on stories, one of which brought them both a certain amount of local fame. A young woman cashier at a downtown ice cream parlor had taken her life because her lover, a gambler by trade, had abandoned her and gone to Miami. Cheney found among her effects a letter piteously setting forth her loneliness.
>
> The next day, her lover, returning from Miami, had gone to the undertaking parlor where the body lay and there shot himself to death over her casket. The undertaker immediately called McGill [who was well known to both the madams and the morticians, his best news sources].
>
> The repentant gambler's suicide added, of course, a new dimension to the story, which McGill made the most of, including the headline that streamed across the top of the front page of the Sunday *Banner*. It was the distraught lover's last words as he held the pistol to his temple: "She killed herself for me. I'll be with her in two minutes."

This was Victorian journalism, with a Victorian af-
termath. There was a house of prostitution about a block
away from the *Banner* office, and when Cheney and
McGill dropped by that Sunday afternoon to buy the
girls a drink, they were still in tears over McGill's story.
"He was," said Cheney, "the hero of the hour". (Martin)

The twenties were an exciting decade for America. Nashville
participated in the Jazz Age and even had a counterpart of New
York's Greenwich Village. Cheney recalls that Nashville had its
own Bohemian community. On the outskirts of the city, high on
top of one of the bluffs overlooking the Cumberland River,
there were several summer camps where various members of
this new Bohemia lived. There was "a syndicated humor col-
umnist, a newspaper reporter or two, a composer, an amateur
painter, librarians, and a few college professors." They all affected an unconventional outlook on life and shunned "the
'bourgeoisie', the church-goers, Rotarians and the country club
set."

I recall that some of us who affected a literary pos-
ture made a creed of Baudelaire's "Be Drunken" and
chanted it, not only on drinking, but many other occasions. I thought then that Ralph best embodied that
commitment to be drunken on "wine, love, or art." With

the footnote that our wine was a pretty raw quality of corn whiskey and our loves were less absorbing than art, under which category we included journalism. ("Notes on Ralph McGill")

In those first years on the *Banner*, encouraged by McGill and Stanley Johnson, Cheney began to write poetry and short stories. Johnson was then an instructor at Vanderbilt and a member of the Fugitive group. He was Cheney's first literary mentor, lending him books about writing, reading his stories, and offering literary advice. In 1927, Johnson published a novel, *The Professor,* that satirized the sometimes dictatorial, sometimes pedantic, Dr. Mims. As a result, he was fired from the University at the end of the term, and joined his comrades, McGill and Cheney, on the *Banner*. Their life was a curious mixture of street reporting, literary discussion, and hard drinking:

To be sure, Houseman was common ground for us then, and Edgar Lee Masters and Edwin Arlington Robinson. But Ralph gave "Miniver Cheevy" and "Mister Flood" special meaning for me through the resonances of his elocution—at times foggy but profound. Oh, we were taken with it all. I recall that Ralph introduced me to Rabelais and for weeks we laughed over and quoted passages about Gargantua to each other.

Most of our literary mouthings were made in was-sail—that is, white lightning colored red. By this time, we thought of it as whiskey and took pride in its relative quality. Our special "source" then was a bootlegger af-fectionately known as "Bull," and he delivered our liq-uor, ordered by phone, to our rooms, hiding the bottle in our bureau drawer for us—and on credit. ("Notes on Ralph McGill")

McGill left the *Banner* for the *Atlanta Constitution* in 1929, but not before acting as best man in Cheney's marriage (June 21, 1928) to Frances Neel of Newbury, South Carolina. Their lives went in separate directions after McGill moved to Atlanta, but they stayed in touch with each other through the years and remained friends until McGill's death in 1969.

During his first years on the *Banner* (1925-28), Cheney was assigned to the police beat. This was one of the toughest as-signments on the paper. It was usually considered the making or breaking ground for the young cub reporter. Cheney's duties were simply to report whatever was happening on the streets. He followed fire trucks whenever they screeched out of the sta-tions; he sometimes rode with policemen, sheriffs and detec-tives as they raided speak-easies, bootleggers, and gambling operations; he checked the hospitals and funeral homes for news-breaking stories; and he attended hours of court sessions, becoming such a steady companion of the judges that they unofficially conferred with him about the dispensation of cases (Cheney, Interview 18 Jan.).

Cheney enjoyed all those duties. He felt he was seeing life up close and becoming acquainted with the reality of his culture and times. He enjoyed the romance of news reporting, and he entered the drama of gathering the news with enthusiasm—sometimes playing his part of hard hitting, dogged reporter with a good deal of ingenuity:

> And then there was the time I interviewed a [notable] patient in a local hospital, wearing a stethoscope and white coat, felt her pulse and advised a free and full confession—and got it, but no real harm done.
>
> One of my most memorable scoops happened when the mistress of a late underworld king (back in 1928) mistook me for C. Vernon Hines, then Assistant District Attorney-General. "Come in, General," she said at the Seventh Avenue, North, doorway. "I been expecting one of y'all all day." I urged her to tell-all, no restraint, and she did, but she spit in my eye when she met me in court three months later.
>
> Memories of those days are happily frescoed with the face of "Sarge" Ed Wright (now Inspector), whose

brusque "Look here, boy" saved my skin more times than prayer. In those days, "Sarge" Wright could quell a mob with a night stick, single-handed—and did so frequently over in Brickyard Bottom.

Incidentally, some years later, he saved my life (or rather my face, which was more important) in the "scaredest" moment of my reportorial stretch. He arrived at the textile mill on the north side of the city just in time to keep 200 striking women—out for horseplay—from stripping me and ducking me in the creek. ("Cheney Leaves Banner Staff")

After three years of reporting on the police beat, he was promoted to political correspondent for the *Banner*. The *Banner* in those days was even more politically partisan than it was later. It often joined hands with the Davidson and Shelby County political machine to support favored candidates. The hottest races in Cheney's career (1927-39) were gubernatorial campaigns. He would be assigned to a particular candidate and travel with him all over the state, reporting his stories back to the *Banner* by phone or, more often in those days, by telegraph.

At the time of his resignation from the *Banner* staff in April of 1940, he wrote an article for the followers of Tennessee politics. In it, he reminisced over the highlights of his twelve years as a political reporter:

Then there was that morning at Jasper when would-be Governor L. E. Gwinn (harassed for expense money in his shoe-string campaign) said as he paced the hotel room, "It looks like I can't go on," and I (with crusading zeal untouched by experience) proposed that we call on the "peepul" to donate (after all we were fighting their cause). This should be amusing to politicians who know the underwritten history of that 1930 campaign.

And Hu Anderson on the floor of the State Senate charging Horton-men with graft and making them like it—the greatest floor leader I ever saw in action, bar none; and Arthur Bruce, Republican gubernatorial candidate, playing Bach to East Tennessee mountaineers, a five-inch cigarette holder in his mouth (you may remember he got the fewest votes a Republican nominee ever got).

The night Carlton Loser lost his race for Congress because the city machine two-timed him and a spokesman offering to trade at 3 a.m. if he would agree to scuttle an anti-machine candidate for the Legislature. But he would not, and he still has my vote as the straightest man I know in the public office. And the three days I spent at the typewriter battling out "leads," first Cheek ahead, then Atkinson, and vice versa and finally Atkinson by thirteen votes.

And Gov. Hill McAlister saying to me in his office during the legislative session of 1935, "But I can't strike at a man who has been my friend for twenty years"—

meaning Crump who had knifed him—a gentleman in an ungentlemanly job. ("Cheney Leaves Banner Staff")

From these experiences and many others like them, Cheney learned the "nuts and bolts" of politics. The revelations were often a shock to his early utopian idealism. He witnessed firsthand the limitations of human nature, and whereas he found a few leaders in those days to believe in, his dominant impression was one of human culpability. He learned that most politicians were driven not by high ideals but by egotism and the opportunity for personal gain. He saw how political bosses could deceptively support one candidate to "split the votes," taking away votes from their opponent and raising the proportionate number of votes of their real choice. And he saw how they could betray a young hopeful by pretending to support him in the early stages of a campaign to discourage other contenders from entering, only to drop him later on in the race.

What effect did all this raw experience have on Cheney? He was often disgusted by what he saw, yet he was also excited to be finally fulfilling part of his early dream—"to participate in the larger world outside of rural Georgia." He became tougher, sometimes cynical, a shrewd analyzer of the political scene. The

Banner called him "the foremost political writer in the State" ("Cheney Leaving Banner to Write").

In Cheney's last four years on the *Banner* staff, he had become interested in writing longer fiction. Years earlier, as a cub reporter, he had written several short stories, with critical help from Stanley Johnson, but now Robert Penn Warren was advising him that it was easier to sell a novel than a short story. In his spare time at night, and on two leaves of absence from the paper, he had written two novels. He did not find a publisher for the first one, but the second one, *Lightwood*, was published and well received. In the spring of 1940, after fifteen years as a journalist, Cheney decided to resign from the *Banner* and to devote the next few years of his life to fiction.

CHAPTER III

The Literary Influence of Caroline Gordon

Since 1920 up until the 1940s, the nation had experienced an unprecedented burst of talent from the South, a renaissance of literature that rivals, and in fiction exceeds, the New England flowering of genius in the 19th century. One has but to look at a list of Southern writers who emerged in this period to be convinced that a renaissance took place—Eudora Welty, Katherine Anne Porter, Thomas Wolfe, Randall Jarrell, James Dickey, Richard Wright, Allen Tate, John Crowe Ransom, William Faulkner, Andrew Lytle, Caroline Gordon, James Agee, Carson McCullers, Flannery O'Connor, Stark Young, William Styron, Jesse Hill Ford, Robert Penn Warren, and others.

These writers were more than regionalists; their influence and significance spread far beyond the South, their works touching the universal in human nature. Yet much of their writing was distinctly Southern—from the South and about the South, its people, traditions, values, and ways of life (Beatty et al. xvi-xxi; Bradbury). Cheney's strongest connection to this Southern Renaissance was through Robert Penn Warren, Allen Tate, and especially Caroline Gordon Tate, from whom he learned the craft of fiction.

In the summer of 1930, Robert Penn Warren returned to America from Oxford University where he had studied for three years as a Rhodes Scholar. After teaching one year at Southwestern College in Memphis, he was appointed in 1931 to the faculty of Vanderbilt University as an assistant professor of English. That year, he and Cheney met and became friends. Cheney and his wife, Frances, were still living on campus in Wesley Hall. Frances had graduated from Vanderbilt in 1928 and was working there full time as a librarian, and Cheney was still a political reporter on the *Nashville Banner*.

Warren and Cheney got along well from the beginning. They were from similar backgrounds—Cheney from rural Georgia and Warren from a tobacco farm in Guthrie, Kentucky—and they were both interested in literature and politics. Most of Cheney's friends during those years were reporters, politicians, and professors from Vanderbilt. The Cheneys enjoyed the social life on the Vanderbilt campus and were frequently visited by the Warrens, who had a small apartment on State Street (Cheney, Interview 18 Feb.).

In 1931, Warren took Cheney over to Clarksville, Tennessee, to meet his friends, Allen Tate and Caroline Gordon Tate. Cheney was tremendously impressed by the Tates. It was an auspicious occasion for him, for in those years that followed, they became his friends, his advisors, and his most important link to the literary world. The Tates had just returned from a three-year sojourn in Paris, and were filled with interesting talk about T. S. Eliot, Herbert Reed, Ford Madox Ford, John Peale Bishop, and the American expatriates, Ernest Hemingway, Gertrude Stein, and her circle of friends. Tate had received a Guggenheim Fellowship in 1928, which had helped to support them in Paris while he worked on the biography, *Jefferson Davis: His Rise and Fall* (Squires 4-5).

The Tates had returned to America, to the South, and were disturbed by the changes that they saw. The concept of the "New South" was beginning to take hold in the country. Northern industries were starting to move southward, and the small farms were beginning to give way to large conglomerates; rural populations were moving to the cities for work. Allen and Caroline were both extremely conservative in their political and economic views, so upon returning, they joined the Vanderbilt Agrarian group who advocated returning to the values, customs, and traditions of the "Old South" (6). The group's views were forcefully articulated in the new classic work, *I'll Take my Stand: The South and the Agrarian Tradition, By Twelve Southerners* (Harper, 1930).

In 1930, the Tates purchased a house near Clarksville, Tennessee and christened it Benfolly. At Benfolly they leased their land to several small farmers on a sharecropping basis and devoted their time to writing, entertaining old friends, and living a simple lifestyle in accord with their agrarian beliefs (Thomson 6). The Cheneys, Warrens, and Tates spent many evenings at Benfolly together. The Cheneys "kept them up" on the political and university life of Nashville, and the Tates reminisced about their years in New York (1924-28) where they had met the literati of the day—Hart Crane, Edmund Wilson, Katherine Anne Porter, Malcolm Cowley—and of their three years in Paris (Cheney, Interview 18 Feb.).

Caroline had been writing for six years. She, like Cheney, had begun as a reporter on the *Chattanooga News* and had later turned to fiction. By 1931, she had published several short stories and one novel, *Penhally*. She was a talented and perceptive writer, with a gift not only for creating fictional worlds but for understanding the theory of her art. Later, she was to publish eight novels and became a nationally acclaimed teacher of creative writing, conducting workshops at Columbia, Purdue, and Princeton.

Cheney had a kindred feeling toward her from the moment of their first meeting. She was only five years his senior, but because of her high intelligence and conservative ways, she seemed much older to him. An interviewer once said that "her conservatism shines like a beacon in everything about her. . . from the way she wears her dark hair, parted in the middle and with a braid encircling her hair. . . [to] the way she prefers simple black dresses with a single gold clip at the neckline" (Ragan 18). Cheney refers to her as his "literary godmother." "She did more for me than any other person. She was a great teacher. She would read my stuff, and we would talk about it. She was also very good about writing out her criticism and suggestions" (Cheney, Interview 18 Feb.).

Caroline Gordon, Cheney's "literary godmother". (*Courtesy Princeton University Library, Department of Rare Books and Special Collections*)

Through the years, Caroline remained Cheney's best literary friend. She taught him the craft of fiction. He already possessed an energetic will and a vivid imagination. She showed him how to harness his energy and turn his sometimes blurred fictional scenes into sharply "rendered" vignettes. In one of her first letters to him, she wrote, "I've taken the liberty of marking up your MS frightfully. There are some things about your style I don't like. (I know from six years' experience that writing newspaper copy corrupts your style.) You use too many big words in this piece. Never say 'resembled' when you can say 'looked alike.' I may be a bad adviser. I have a sort of mania for exactness in prose. But if you're writing fiction, you must make it as vivid, as concrete as you can, and to do that, you must say everything as directly as possible. This is all I can think of, and I doubt if any of it is much help. But if I ever can be of any help about anything concerned with writing, I'll be very glad to" (Gordon, "To Brainard Cheney" March 1932).

Their exchange of 120 letters over the years is a remarkable literary testimonial of their relationship. The letters are preserved in the Special Collections Department of Vanderbilt University. The letters chronicle a friendship that lasted over forty years, and they show in detail the manner in which she helped him learn the techniques of fiction and the ways of the literary world. She became his literary mentor—his advisor, teacher, critic, and friend. She taught him about dialogue:

> I think your conversation on the whole is good. You seem to have grasped instinctively a theory that many modern writers have about dialogue: that it is used chiefly for the purpose of creating reality and not to convey information, except in moments of dramatic crisis. Hemingway's dialogue, if you will notice, is very cunningly written to give the sound of speech ringing in a room. I myself always test every speech I write, reading it aloud to see if it *sounds* as if somebody has just said it. (Gordon, "To Brainard Cheney" 9 Feb.)

> [About interior monologue:] I suppose you know what the interior monologue is (character talking to himself shall we say?) I should think you'd have to use it—I use it too much. Red Warren never uses it, having a feeling against it, but he says each sentence he writes in a novel is like butting his head against a stone wall. The advantage of the interior monologue is that it gives depth and therefore the illusion of reality. If the author records only what the man says and does, we have a flat picture of him—the interior monologue goes in behind him so that we see him in the round. (Gordon, "To Brainard Cheney" 12 March)

In her own writing, Gordon was greatly influenced by Percy Lubbock's *The Craft of Fiction*, the Prefaces of Henry James, and the realistic techniques of Gustave Flaubert. She passed on to Cheney her theories about how a novel exists and how it is sustained. Gordon's ideas about fiction were later published in an anthology that she co-authored with her husband, Allen Tate, *The House of Fiction* (1950) and in her own book of fictional criticism, *How to Read a Novel* (1957). She wrote to Cheney explaining:

> A novel is a series of camera shots. . . .The photographer walks around his subject and figures what will be the best angle. You have to do almost the same thing in writing a chapter. You have certain things to get over. You have to arrange them so that the action will run off like a movie film. You can't just tell the reader that certain things happened. You have to make them happen, and this involves triggering with events so that action will be continuous. . . .The basic reason for this is that anything seen in a novel has more emotional impact if seen by one of the characters. You can describe a tree, but it will be more real as a tree if you have one of your characters see the tree and then give the reader the tree in terms of what it was to that character. To press the analysis further, the tree and the character help each other exist. (Gordon, "To Brainard Cheney" 31 Oct.)

In another letter, she continued:

> It is difficult, of course, to say just what writing con-
> sists of, but certainly you can reduce it to two major op-
> erations in the mind. You conjure up a scene—and if you
> are good, it will be real enough to obscure reality for the
> time being. You then describe what you see, as exactly as
> you can. How good your stuff is will depend first on how
> powerful your imagination is and next on how exactly
> you describe things. Don't try for literary effects. Dreiser
> is one of the most powerful writers in the country, and
> he can't write a decent sentence to save his neck. Just be
> sure you see something and then get it in (Gordon, "To
> Brainard Cheney" 12 March).

She also gave him excellent advice about the literary markets and when he might publish his material: "I should recommend that you can send it [his first novel] first to Coward-
McCann and then to Stokes. I have another suggestion. You
might try it first on an agent. This simplifies matters considerably, as you don't have to bother with sending it around. The
big agents, my own, for instance, are almost as hard to make as
publishers. And as a matter of fact, the small agents, ones who
take only a few books and peddle them personally, do just as
well for you in the long run, I believe. I suggest that you send it
to Nannine Joseph, a girl I know and have confidence in. Her

address is 200 West Fifty Fourth Street. She won't take it unless she thinks she can sell it. I enclose a note to her which you can put in with the manuscript" (Gordon, "To Brainard Cheney" 9 Feb.).

"You are going to run into the usual difficulty one has in writing a story of the South. Yankee reviewers always complain of the multiplicity of characters; they do not realize that a Southern scene is always crowded. The only thing you can do is try to individualize your characters. Do not introduce any character that you do not need and try to make each one stand out as a personality" (Gordon, "To Brainard Cheney" 12 March).

She recommended books for him to read and study. "What you ought to do—if you intend to go on writing novels—is to study some of the great novels. Take them to pieces and see how they are put together. 'Madam Bovary,' for instance, would certainly reward you. Dostoyevsky's 'Crime and Punishment' starts out as your book does with a man making a misstep which brings his fate upon him. Of course, the Russians are dangerous food. Anything they do is all so mixed up with the Russian soul—they are all soul—that it is difficult to disentangle the threads of the narrative from the exuberance. Read Hardy's 'Tess of the d'Urbervilles.' Keep off 'War and Peace' for a while, anyhow. It wouldn't do you any harm to study Hemingway, for his beautiful sense of form and for his dialogue" (Gordon, "To Brainard Cheney" 9 Feb.). In addition to her comments about fictional techniques and theory, Gordon also gave close readings with editorial suggestions to each page of his manuscript.

> I append some little things I thought needed changing:

> Page 8 "though she were keen scented" doesn't sound just right. "No matter how keen scented he was?"
> Page 9: "his theory of integrity." You can hardly have a *theory* of integrity. His sense of integrity?
> 18: "practical moral." Do you mean moral code? The idea is good, but you can't say practical moral.
> 20: "You see it's time for me to be unwell." I am not sure, not knowing just what market the book may make, whether you have to skate carefully. Better say sick. Or no, leave it and let the publisher worry over that one.
> 29: This paragraph about his grandfather and the next two paragraphs that follow it are the best in the book. This is really good writing. The description of the grandfather is fine, and the paragraph about the girl squatting on the pile of cottonseed is just as good and extremely dramatic.

99: Nancy wouldn't spell "Papa" "Popper." You're taking an unfair advantage of her there. Better make it "Papa." (Gordon, "To Brainard Cheney" 9 Feb.)

Caroline Gordon helped many other Southern writers over the years, especially in the early stages of their careers (Andrew Lytle, Flannery O'Connor, and Walker Percy, for example), and they have much for which to thank her. Her contribution to Southern Letters should someday be researched and documented, for she was truly a gifted artist and a great teacher.

Cheney profited enormously from her advice, but it should not be assumed that she was his only source of criticism. Robert Penn Warren read and criticized all of his works, Andrew Lytle, a good portion of them, and Flannery O'Connor, who through Gordon's introduction, became a life-long friend and confidant, read and made suggestions on the early drafts of three of his novels, two plays, and most of his literary essays and reviews. Over the years their friendship and mutual criticism produced an exchange of 188 letters captured in Ralph Stephens' *The Correspondence of Flannery O'Connor and the Brainard Cheneys*. His editors, Paul Brooks of Houghton Mifflin Company and David McDowell of McDowell, Obolensky, also read his manuscripts and offered suggestions.

Flannery O'Connor (seated at the right) on one of her many visits to Idler's Retreat, pictured with Frances and Brainard Cheney. *(Courtesy Vanderbilt University Special Collections)*

Cheney learned a great deal from these sources of criticism, especially from Caroline Gordon, but he learned most from his own creative "travail"—trying to make his words reveal the visions of his mind. In 1949, he wrote a letter to the novelist Harold Davis that reveals how he tempered the critical advice from his friends with his own independent thought.

Recently, Red (R. P.) Warren was by to see me, talking about the novel "as discourse"—and I, at the moment, trying to get on with his current one, WORLD ENOUGH AND TIME. Red was not able, in the allotted time, to convey to me what he means by the novel as discourse—if, indeed, he yet knows—a thing, I suspect, he is trying to find out for himself—which, to be sure, is commendable. Neither did his novel do so—in fact, it left me on first reading as uncertain as our discussion—I admit that I suffered undue interruption and was too much preoccupied to analyze the difficulties it presented for me at the time. I've been laying off to read it again but haven't got to it—what is your opinion of it?

Then he was followed almost immediately by Allen and Caroline Tate, who think the idea of a novel as a discourse is bosh and that Red has gone to the bowwows by this last book. They too had out a new book, called *The House of Fiction*—notably not a creative work, but an anthology with critical notes—all in the traditional Jamesean view.

I haven't had the time or leisure to come to grips with the technical theories of either faction—I'm not even sure what the opposition is, but at first blush, both leave me unsatisfied. For example, it seems to me that the analogies we use for describing the more abstract and the less abstract representation of experience can be pressed too far—I mean the distinctions conveyed by summary vs. scene, panorama vs. drama and, in her usage, Long View vs. Short View—which seems to me to imply the most extreme photographic preconception. (Cheney, "To Harold Davis")

The letters in the Cheney Papers of the Special Collections Department of Vanderbilt University are a pleasure to read. They contain a wealth of information about how writers help each other, the ins and outs of publishing, details of personal friendships, and literary opinions. In addition to the exchange of letters with Caroline Gordon, the Cheney Papers include several hundred letters to Flannery O'Connor, Robert Penn Warren, Walker Percy, and many other Southern writers. This literary treasure of correspondence gives one a sense of what it was like to be alive and writing during the South's literary renaissance.

CHAPTER IV

Lightwood

A Novel of the Land Battles of Post-Civil War Georgia, 1870-1890

World Beyond Words

As a boy, Brainard Cheney had dreamed of someday becoming a writer. He had always possessed an active imagination, and he had enjoyed listening to the stories of Robin Bess and the old-timers around Lumber City. His years of work on the *Banner* had broken him into print, and he had from time to time written a few short stories. As he became better friends with the Tates in the early 1930s, Caroline had begun reading his stories and giving him literary advice. She liked his work but felt that the short story was too confining a medium for him. Both she and Robert Penn Warren suggested that he try writing a novel.

With their support and encouragement, Cheney decided to try to realize his old ambition of becoming a writer; he began his first novel in 1933. Since he was still working on the *Banner*, he had to confine his fiction writing to nights and weekends. It took him three years to finish *World Beyond Words*, and it never was published, but it was a beginning for him as a novelist. *World Beyond Words* is a realistic, gutsy story about a young man's struggle to find his place in society. Wentworth Ball is principal of a small, rural school in Cauld's Junction, Georgia. Determined to rise above this position, he attends the University of Georgia during the summer, hoping to earn a law degree and to set up his own practice. As a boy, he was raised in a genteel Southern tradition, and his Victorian mother watched with encouragement his climb to success. He was engaged to a refined, Southern girl of whom his mother approved, and at the beginning of the novel, his future looked bright and promising.

Cheney uses Wentworth's mother and the young girl as symbols of tradition, respectability, reason, and logic. As a counterforce to these elements in the young man's life, Cheney creates the character, Nancy Plumber.

Nancy is a young teacher on the staff of the school, and, as was the case in many rural schools in those days, she has little more than a high school education herself. Coming from a poor family, she has little grace or charm in her personal manners. However, she is very attractive and seductive. The young principal, high-minded and success-oriented, yields to the power of his glands. The following passage reveals Wentworth's psychological dilemma—the clash of forces within him between reason and desire, traditional values and reality.

> But, suddenly from somewhere in his being a low spark flared. He felt a slight swinging within his viscera. Blood pressed his skin. The train of his thinking snapped. . .He told himself it was the mere lust of a dog—that he need make no mystery of it—he told himself that he was weak as water—that he was acting a stupid simpleton! He buttressed himself with reason and moral law, with sensibility and sentiment against another such collapse. But, he was not sure of his will, or the force of his logic. (Cheney, *World Beyond Words* 43)

Cheney tells the story in a hard, unromantic manner. The philosophical undercurrent of the action is similar to the naturalism of Theodore Dreiser; the plot is much like his *An American Tragedy* of 1925. Wentworth, like Clyde Griffiths, is torn between his desire for success and his passion for a woman who can only hurt him socially.

In Cheney's novel, Nancy becomes pregnant, and there are long grisly scenes of an abortion episode—locating a disreputable doctor, arranging the time and place, enduring moral and physical fear, the operation, and recovery. The following passage from that sequence demonstrates the realistic tone of the novel and Cheney's power of rendering a scene:

He [Wentworth] became conscious of the fact that the curtain, drab with dust, divided the room into inner and outer offices. There now issued from behind it the sound of voices, sharp-edged and inarticulate—a man and woman argued. He could not identify a single article in the outer office with a doctor. On the square topped table lay a grayish, cloth-bound book that appeared to be a ledger. Two empty glass jugs stood against the wall across the room. A pencil-scrawled calendar hung on the wall, discolored by leaks and gray with dust.

[The doctor,] now approaching him, removed a weather-stained derby, uncovering dirty yellowish white hair. He came at a slow gait on legs that seemed uncertain of sustaining him and smiled with a ghostly unction. Wentworth felt his eyes widening and lines about his mouth tightening as the man came close. There was a faint trace of professional convention about his clothes, but they were faded into no recognizable color and threadbare. Wentworth was not conscious of having seen his clothes: his face! Bloodless, puffy, inanimate—it had the look of soggy dough that has been kneaded by dirty hands. . . .

The man never answered his question about the operation, but it became evident that an answer was not necessary. Dealing with strangers in such operations he must take precautions, he said. Did the young man expect to pay for it himself? And, was he able to pay cash? Wentworth asked the amount, yes. Heavy lids lifted a little and the yellowish eyes were briefly animate coming finally to rest on Wentworth's shoes—the fee would be twenty-five dollars. But, in such cases he always required a down payment. The eyes were lifted again for a moment. He must have five dollars now—just a precaution to be certain the client kept his appointment. (58-62)

The abortion sequence takes up one-third of the story because the unwanted life is a symbol of nature's way of thwarting Wentworth's plans. It is not until this obstacle is removed that Wentworth reaches a resolution in his mind about his life. Ironically, he forsakes his old Southern sweetheart and returns to Nancy. They had suffered much together, and this suffering plus their natural attraction overcomes tradition, logic, and his desire to succeed.

World Beyond Words was a rugged, stark novel for 1937, and the narration was not always very accomplished, yet it was a powerful story. Caroline Gordon thought that it was good for a first novel:

> I am favorably impressed by your novel. I read it yesterday, almost at one sitting, and I found myself staying up late to finish it, not because I was anxious to get the job done but because I was genuinely interested to see how it would turn out. You have a good grasp of character and structure, and those, of course, are the all important things (Gordon, "To Brainard Cheney" 9 Feb.).

However, Miss Gordon's agent in New York, Nannine Joseph, was not optimistic about the chances of selling it; she returned the manuscript to him, saying:

> I rather have a feeling that it's very definitely your first novel, not only first to be offered, but first that you have written, and that it would be wiser to put it aside and consider it merely as an exercise in learning the technique, and wait for the second one, because you *can* write (Joseph, "To Brainard Cheney" 10 March).

Cheney wasn't terribly disappointed by the news because he had proven to himself that he could write an extended narrative, and Caroline had seemed not only impressed by his effort but committed to helping him in any way she could. He was also eager to begin work on a new idea for a novel, one that had come to him while he was finishing *World Beyond Words*.

Lightwood

In the fall of 1936, Cheney, having received a leave of absence from the *Banner*, went to Lumber City, Georgia, to complete the writing of *World Beyond Words*. Because his family no longer lived there—his mother had died years before in 1925, and his sisters were married and living elsewhere—he took a small room in the Ocmulgee Hotel, one of the town's few hotels. It took him two months in that small hotel room to rework and complete the novel. After he finished it, he decided to relax for a while and visit some of his old friends and relatives.

On one of his visits with his second cousin, Tom McCrae, who was the mill superintendent for the W. E. Dodge Lumber Company, they began reminiscing about the South, the Reconstruction era, and the land conflicts between the lumber companies and the backwoodsmen of Georgia. After a few hours of talk, McCrae took Cheney to a room filled with stacks of documents recording the Company's early land negotiations. He told him that if he were interested, he could look through them as much as he wanted. Cheney dug into the records and emerged two weeks later with the idea for a historical novel (Cheney, Interview 18 Feb.). He originally called it *The Squatters* but later changed the title to *Lightwood*, his first published novel.

In *Lightwood*, Cheney recreates in fiction the frontier history of South Georgia, the country of his youth, the region of the South that he was born into, loved, and eventually left. The action takes place over a sixteen-year period, from 1874 to 1890; through the use of flashbacks, it goes back even further, to 1810 when Georgia first purchased the lands between the Ocmulgee and Oconee rivers from the Indians. The farmers who came to settle these lands suffered great hardships. They cleared homesteads out of wilderness, fighting disease, drought, poverty, and hostile Indians.

After the Civil War, large Northern land companies moved into the impoverished South, buying up land by the thousands of acres at extremely low prices. The land they couldn't buy they took from the frontier squatters through costly and complex litigation. Under Georgia law, the land belonged to the frontiersmen by right of having settled it and possessing it for

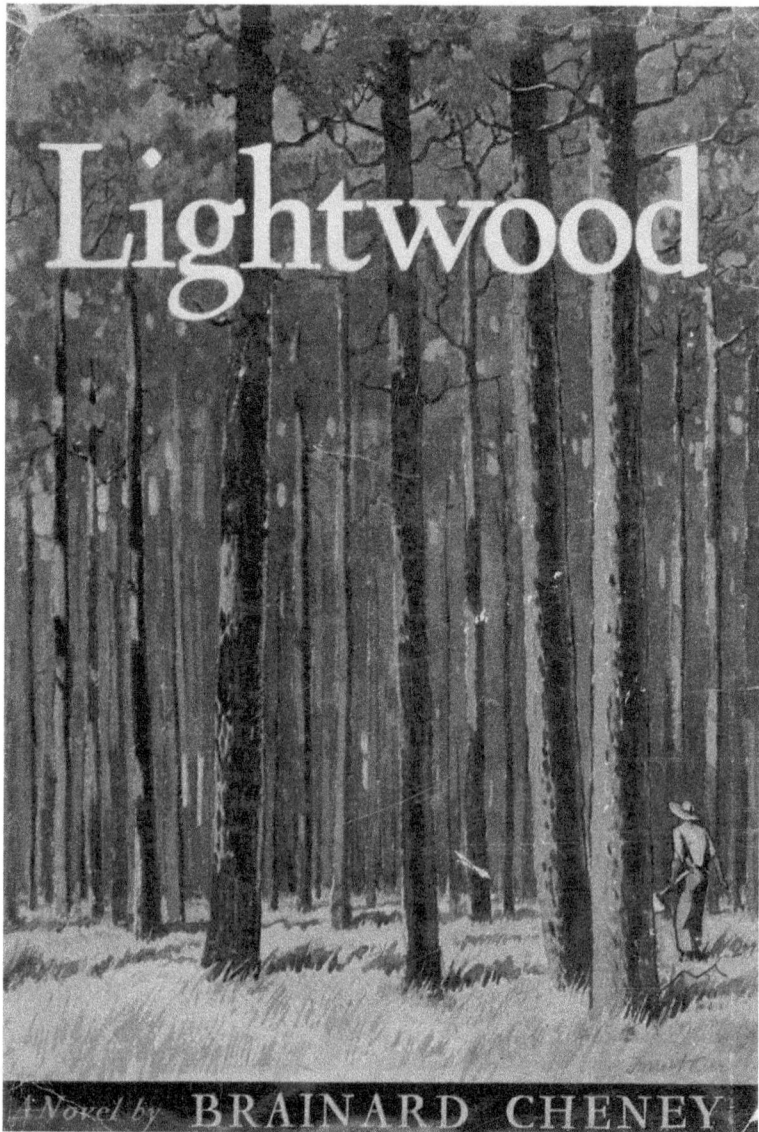

Cheney's first novel, *Lightwood*, appeared in 1939. Received with favorable reviews nationally, it sold modestly. The novel fictionalized a story of the Dodge Land Wars in South Georgia during a period from 1870 through 1890. The cover was by artist Forrest Orr.

twenty years. This law, however, was superseded in the Federal courts that favored Northern industry. The South, poor, depressed, and agrarian, could not resist this second invasion from the North. As to the relation of his novel to events in Georgia history, Cheney says, "I only attempted to use this as a background, though my story, I think, is essentially a sound interpretation of what happened. Everything in the particular is fictional: the characters, the incidents, the episodes. . . .The only thing I have followed closely and faithfully is the legal history." (Cheney, Rev. of *Lightwood*).

Though *Lightwood* chronicles a particular conflict in South Georgia, it is representative of similar struggles throughout the South during the years of Reconstruction. In comparing the South to a defeated foreign nation, whose people have to recover on terms set by the enemy, Richard Weaver writes, "The way in which the South was systematically bled in the decades following the war has been set forth by Southern historians. . .It is enough to point out that a recovery which under favorable conditions might have required ten or fifteen years required more than fifty and actually cannot be regarded as complete yet." (Rubin and Jacobs 25).

Cheney chooses one family to symbolize what many Southern families endured, much as John Steinbeck used the Joad family in *The Grapes of Wrath* to reveal the hardships of the farmers in Oklahoma during the Depression.

The Georgia family that Cheney follows is named Corn, and the patriarch of that family is Micajah Corn. Cheney begins the story by presenting a picture of Micajah at home reflecting on the past and wondering if the information he had received the day before was true, if the new land company had his land marked for confiscation on their surveying maps.

> Micajah Corn sat in a duck-legged chair before the fire in the big double-pen house on Cedar Creek. Behind him the great square room was dim with wavering shadows, but the circle of firelight was bright. On the wall above the mantel was stretched a catamount skin. The chair Micajah sat on had a deer-hide bottom. The hide had been worn slick and black by years of sliding backsides, but the chair was still Micajah's favorite. He tilted it forward now and, carefully picking up a blazing splinter from the hearth, lighted his pipe.
>
> The flaring splinter revealed a long man whose body had the lean, twisted look of an ironwood tree. His graying hair almost brushed his shoulders. His face was complacent yet melancholy. The gray-streaked, yellowish mustache, curving down over his lips, then gently

upward to loosely twisted ends, gave the illusion of a fixed, mild smile. (Cheney, *Lightwood* 1)

After telling his family about the disturbing news, Micajah decides to go to Lancaster, the county seat, with his aging father and two of his sons to confront the Coventry land company and to warn them not to send surveyors to his land. He knows that Georgia law gives him claim to the land, and he plans to keep it, with or without the help of the courts.

Before the Corns reach Lancaster, however, they unexpectedly have their first in a long series of confrontations with Coventry Company. Cheney uses the company's train as a symbol of the coming industrialism. The Corns, like the Indians of Mexico upon seeing for the first time the charging horses of the invading Spaniards, are overwhelmed by the might of the Coventry locomotive as it blasts through the quietness of their agrarian life:

> . . . the sun was swinging low toward the tree line, when they heard it. It wasn't much of a noise at first, just a faraway rumble above the wash of the pines. Then it was a racket, like a big wind coming up from behind along the railroad clearing. The Corns could not see down the clearing because of the trees, but the roaring was coming on terrifically fast. It was like nothing Little-

ton had ever heard before. It grew louder, louder, louder. His eardrums seemed about to break, his head buzzed. The horses began to run. Micajah grabbed the lines and tried to saw them down, for the road now ran close to the tracks.

A black locomotive, spewing steam and smoke, rounded the bend with its wind-rifled coaches and hurtled along the clearing toward them. It came on, right at them—like a steamboat boiler shot out of a gun. (10)

At first, the company tries to be amicable in their dealings with the backwoodsmen, but after they lose a few battles over land titles in the Georgia courts, they become ruthless. Through legal maneuvers, the company is able to move their title debates to the Federal Courts in Savannah and Macon. There, they receive favorable rulings from bought judges. With the law on their side, the company hires and deputizes gunmen to run the squatters off the land.

After Micajah sees that the battle through the courts is lost, he turns to the unwritten laws of the frontier. His training as a woodsman and soldier help him strike serious blows at the company. He and his sons set fire to lumber mills, sabotage timber rafts on the river, and help their neighbors who have received eviction notices to defend their homesteads. In the end, however, he is beaten. He loses two sons and several relatives, and his land is finally taken from him. The power of the companies, their wealth and influence, especially their ability to use Federal Courts to obtain legal rights to the land, is too great.

Cheney achieves a number of successes in the telling of *Lightwood*—successes in describing frontier life and recording rural dialects, successes in narrative technique and character development. He shows us the homes, the farms, the pine woods and rural towns of South Georgia. We see what the Georgia backwoodsman looks like, how he acts, and how he thinks. We are drawn to these simple but rugged people, and we endure their hardships and share their hopes for the future. Cheney describes their heroism, but he does it without sentimentality or romance, for the backwoodsmen were as rough and crude as they were noble.

The following passage, quoted at length, demonstrates Cheney's skill in creating scenes that make these frontier people come to life. His mastery of the cadence, dialect, and folk idioms of the Georgian speech adds to the realism of these scenes. After the Federal Court rules in favor of the Coventry Company, the backwoodsmen hold a meeting in a local blacksmith's shop to decide what to do:

A group of men stood in a semi-circle at a short dis-
tance from the forge and others squatted or stood beneath each of the torches. They were men of bushy
beards and hair, most of them, and with cheekbones
sharpened and eyes glinted by the firelight. They quietly
swapped chews of tobacco and talked two or three in a
group.

Soon after Micajah arrived, Ben Cameron, his jowls
as clean-shaven as a town man's, stood up from the anvil
against which he had been leaning and said, "Men, I
reckon we'd better start this thing." Those about the
forge backed off a little and many of them squatted
down. "I'll get the talking started," he continued, "and
we'll hear from everybody who's got anything to say.

Cameron then called out the name of Merlin, and a
thickset, swart man with heavy black hair and beard
stood up. He spoke in a booming voice. "Men, have you
a-heard this un?" he began, and then he said Zenas
Fears had run Rube Faulk and the Dopson boys off their
land that morning. Rube and the Dopsons had stopped a
crew of Coventry's niggers come out to cut their timber.
The niggers had stopped, but in a little while Fears had
come up with two henchmen. Fears had told them, the
way Merlin heard it, to go get a court paper if they wanted to stop the choppers. And Rube had 'lowed he'd shoot
any man who put an axe in his timber. Then Fears and
his men had pulled their guns and bluffed Rube and the
Dopsons off.

The black-bearded man sat down and an old hunch-
back, with hair growing out of his ears and a goat-like

beard, said shrilly: "that un makes the twelfth—he's put twelve families off'n their land around here in Telfair County since April. Men, Coventry don't aim to stop nowhere this time—he'll cut anybody's timber—anywhere now!" There was widespread shifting of feet among the men standing and spitting, and many of the listeners nodded at each other . . .

A voice spoke out, "Who's a-goin' to handle the crowd? How we a-goin' about it, Micajie?"

Micajah turned back from the forge and, pausing, took off his hat. The fire threw his long wavering shadow before him. "It don't need no crowd," he said. "Idees can be passed back'ards and fo'ards through the shops here. Every man can work with his own crowd. Any crowd knows its men. What they do they can a-keep close. We'll all a-know what's goin' on after it happens." Here he paused and looked deliberately from side to side and out to the edge of the group. "There won't be any stray ears to a-hear things, naer stray mouths to a-spread talk about it."

He turned again to the firelight. The crowd broke into small clots. The men of each group talked quietly among themselves. Micajah told Cameron he guessed he'd be going. A gruff voice at his elbow spoke up a little louder than the level of the conversation. "Who air ye a-goin' to work with, Micajie?"

Micajah looked sharply at the man. After a pause he turned back toward the fire as if he did not intend to reply, but he spoke to the flames. "There's still enough Corns left to be heard from." (199-204)

Time Magazine praised Cheney's narrative skills, especially his successes in writing scenes of violence that are free of melodrama.

> With a constant and expert attentiveness to exactitudes of speech, gesture, action, he writes of violence (a negress cutting a white man's throat), horror (a father incapable of restraining his vomit over the 10-day corpse of his son), brutality (a man's foot pinning a fighting woman to the earth by her pregnant belly), without any slackening into the merely melodramatic. He achieves all this in a dulled, plainfeatured, transparent prose. (*Time* 71)

In one violent scene in the book, Cheney reveals his growing mastery of narrative technique. *Lightwood* is told from an omniscient point of view, with the narrator usually following very closely the thoughts and actions of his main characters. Once, however, to achieve a special effect, he stands far away from a character. In the last third of the novel, an assassin is hired to murder Ian McIntosh, the general superintendent of Coventry Company. As the murderer moves mysteriously and anonymously toward his victim, Cheney's narrator describes his actions in a correspondingly distant and objective tone.

He moved deliberately, but with sure direction, and in less than an hour he was out of the woods and within sight of the lights of Pineville.

The mist had given way to a downpour. The man hesitated at the edge of the woods. He felt briefly the long oilcloth-wrapped bundle he carried and then moved on through the night rain like a shadow.

He moved swiftly now in the direction of the light. He stopped at the edge of the oblong and looked in through the window. Then he pivoted his head and looked around him. Rain still fell in a noisy downpour and rolled from the eaves of the porch in a ragged edge. He shifted away from the light and approached the porch edge.

Leeched close to the shadow he faced the window. In the half-light, his face was a dull snuff color. Nothing about him took sharp form except the gun barrel beside his leg and his eyes. They were still ovals of white.

The room within the window was softly lighted from the ceiling. Around the walls were open bookshelves of light brown wood. And a glow came from a fireplace beside the window. There was a long low table and on one end of it rested a green-shaded reading-lamp. Within the cone of lamplight was a large, slanted-backed easy-chair, upholstered darkly. A large man filled the chair. A fresh cigar smoked in his fingers and his gaze was on the newspaper in his hands. His firm cheeks were a reddish color. Above, his forehead shone white, except for a gray curving lock of hair. He was alone in the room.

All of this the eyes took in, though they were still but a moment. Then the gun barrel came up, paused for an infinite fraction of time, and spurted flame. There was a detonation and a splintering of glass through the dull roar of the rain. Then the porch was empty. The man was gone. (Cheney, *Lightwood* 315-317)

The creation of Micajah Corn is Cheney's greatest success in *Lightwood*. Through Micajah, Cheney portrays his most important and recurring subject—the drama of the insufficient hero. Cheney creates Micajah, a frontier Georgian of heroic dimensions, to fight against the overpowering forces of an epic moment: the invasion of Northern industry into the South. When Micajah is inevitably beaten, his loss becomes not only a personal defeat but a symbol of the tragic fate of the South.

Micajah is one of the best of the Georgian backwoodsmen. He is a man of strength and courage who, though unlettered, possesses a sharp mind. He had sprung from ancestors who had settled the wilderness of Georgia, and their knowledge of the woods and ways of making the land yield a living were passed on to him. Yet Micajah's vision and understanding of the world is limited to his surroundings. He knows nothing of nor cares for the larger conflicts with which the nation struggles. When the Civil War comes, it is of no concern to him until one of his sons is killed in battle. That personal attack makes the war meaningful to him, and he joins the fighting, not for a vague, abstract cause but to find the man who had killed his son:

> Then look at me when word come that they had killed Kinch up in Maryland! I acted just like a cow smelling blood. Thinking I could take my flint-and-steel and walk up on 'em somewhere and get their scalps! And taking poor Clute with me. I reckon he'd've joined up anyhow, if I'd left him, though. He had the same sort of fool in him. Maryland! I didn't even see it. I didn't even get in the same army. And the first shooting I got into was at a town called Murfreesboro way over in Tennessee.
>
> There was plenty to shoot at all right, and plenty shooting at ye. I had a pretty good rifle they gave me— for a while. I seen it drop 'em, too. And at first I thought it was pretty fine. But by that time another year I was sick of it. At Dalton and at Resaca, where they winged me. Them poor devils hadn't ever heard of Kinch and didn't know me from Adam's haw steer. They hadn't come to get me, either—just mixed up in it, like I was. (50)

The struggle to retain his land is like another Civil War. Once again he experiences the agony of being wronged and not knowing whom to blame. The impersonal land corporation and federal courts are as hard to fight as the unknown soldier who had killed his son. The men who came to run him off his land are not personal enemies. They are agents in an industrial machine. When he is victorious over them, they are automatically replaced by others. Coventry Land Company is a mechanical Hydra with an infinite number of replaceable heads.

Ultimately, Micajah is beaten. The forces of industrialism that come to his land are too powerful. But it is not that alone that destroys him. He is undone as well by his pride and the corruption that develops in his family from fifteen years of fighting. Micajah knows that God didn't hold with killing, yet for years, he hates and tries to kill Zenas Fears, one of the company's ruffians. Zenas had killed one of Micajah's sons who was trying to protect a neighbor from being run off his land. Micajah, in turn, had vowed to kill Zenas, but bad luck haunts the task. He shoots at him twice, once with a pistol as Zenas approaches him on horseback—the bullet meant for his chest, absorbed by a padded protective vest—and again years later, with a shotgun as Zenas rounds a bend in the road with his posse. Micajah is too far away; the shots that hit Zenas do no permanent damage. Micajah, in contempt for his bad luck, curses God.

As a heroic warrior, Micajah keeps himself pure through the years of fighting. He stays close to his values and his frontier codes of honor. He only fights back when the company advances. If they eject his neighbors, he burns their mills. When they kill a friend, he sabotages their timber rafts. When they kill his son, he goes after the company man who did the shooting.

The members of his family and other backwoodsmen, however, do not remain unsullied from the years of conflict. They become as ruthless as the land company. Some of Micajah's relatives accept compromise and employment in the company's lumber mills. A second son of Micajah's is killed stealing rafts of timber in a time when the company was not pressing their claims, and a third son is persuaded by Calhoun Caleb, a lawyer and distant cousin of Micajah's, to join a conspiracy to murder Ian McIntosh, Coventry Company's general superintendent. In Micajah's code of warfare, assassination is base and ignoble. Besides, McIntosh is not even a "Yankee." He is a Canadian, who through fairness and courage had won the respect of many of the backwoodsmen.

Each corrupting act of his family strikes against Micajah's will to continue the long heroic struggle. The final blow comes to him when he learns that Jasmine, his unmarried and favored daughter, is carrying the child of Calhoun Caleb, the same man who had corrupted his son. The family's personal depravities and tragedies (two sons dead, a third corrupted, and a daughter dishonored)—in addition to his inability to stop Zenas Fears and the advancing Coventry Company—all strike Micajah at once. Cursing God in impotent rage, "He threw the hammer from him. He felt his palm tingle as the handle left it. Then the tingling spread, up into his neck. There was a prickling in his right cheek. He looked down and saw that his right arm was hanging by his side. There was a prickling in his leg. He was falling to the ground" (340).

Micajah's stroke leaves him defeated and broken; half his body is paralyzed, and he can no longer walk without assistance. From this point in the novel, he no longer functions as the defiant hero. He has been tested, tried, and found insufficient to the struggle. But Cheney is not through with him yet, as the North was not through with the South after the war. As a symbol of both the falling hero and the tragic South, Micajah, like the South during the Reconstruction Era, must suffer further humiliations.

After the assassination of McIntosh, Coventry Company tries without success to bring the murderers to justice. Micajah, now only half a man, believing that God had punished him for his part in the fight and that he must atone for his sins, testifies against his son and Calhoun Caleb. The company welcomes Micajah's help and promises him a clear title to his land.

After the trial, which is held in the Federal Court in Macon, Micajah returns to McRae by train. While waiting for one of his kinsmen to pick him up for a wagon ride back to his homestead, he stops at a local café for something to eat. As Micajah sits drinking a cup of coffee and thinking about finally being able to farm his land again in peace, he is approached by a new agent of Coventry Company:

"You're Micajah Corn, ain't you?" he said; then, without awaiting a reply, looked at a slip of paper in his hand. "You been making a claim to lot 180?"

Micajah lowered his saucer and nodded slowly.

The man looked down at his paper. "Lots 180, 181, 145, and 146 in the Seventh District, and lot 47 in the Fifth?" He read the numbers briskly, following the line on the sheet with his finger. He raised his eyes and peered at Micajah and Civil through his thick lenses. "You're just the man I'm looking for, Mr. Corn. You make the eighty-ninth. I got four hundred of these to serve before I get through."

Micajah opened his mouth, but he did not speak.

The man handed Micajah the slip of paper. "Served eighty-eight of these summons in the last six days," he said. He stood a moment with his hands on his hips, rocking back on his heels. "The company's bundled the whole lot of land cases into one ejectment suit. They're going to try it in the Macon Court."

Micajah fumbled with the piece of paper in his hand. He lowered his gaze, but he did not look at the paper. He stared beyond the man, at the counter, at the cup that still sat there full of coffee.

"Macon?" he said. "Macon Court." (368-369)

In this grimly ironic ending, Cheney underscores the trage- dy of the South—beaten in the Civil War and defeated in the peace of Reconstruction. It is as if he were saying that the best the South could produce, a native frontiersman like Micajah Corn with his heroic qualities of honor, pride, intelligence and will, was not sufficient to stem the tide of history, to hold back the invading forces of Northern industry.

The Houghton-Mifflin Company published *Lightwood* in the fall of 1939 and launched a strong advertising campaign to make it a big seller. They were very impressed with the novel and had chosen it as runner-up in their annual Literary Achievement Award (Brooks, "To Brainard Cheney" May 1939).

In *The Taster's Cup*, a trade journal sent to libraries and bookstores, the editors of Houghton-Mifflin described the novel in glowing and dramatic terms:

> This is a novel of the Georgia Pine Barrens and of the men who lived on them when they were covered by virgin timber. These men were part farmer, part hunter, and part animal in their uncanny knowledge of the forest.
>
> There is in it, also, a new indomitability. The book is the history of a magnificent struggle between the forest men and the lumber companies, in which one finds the forest men playing their desperate hands as shrewdly and recklessly as if it were a game of poker. "Lightwood" is a book that should be widely read and greatly enjoyed by everyone who enjoys the best in modern American writing. (32-33)

When the Tates learned that Houghton-Mifflin was going to publish his novel, they were thrilled, and Caroline proudly claimed her part in the victory. "Hooray!!! Allen and I are both so excited and pleased over the news. Wish you'd got the thousand but two fifty now and two fifty later are good enough. And being announced as runner-up will be good publicity. I freely take all the credit you or anybody else will hand me over this job. I feel sure I performed an indispensable service. At a certain stage in the game you just have to have somebody tell you your stuff is good. A wife or mother or maiden aunt will do. But of course it is better if you have somebody who knows a little about what you are trying to do. I am very glad I was on hand at the right moment. I really am awfully proud" (Gordon, "To Brainard Cheney" 26 May).

Cheney celebrates publication of his first novel, *Lightwood*, at Zibart's Bookstore in Nashville, Fall of 1939. (*Courtesy Vanderbilt University Special Collections*)

Lightwood was widely and favorably reviewed in the press and in magazines. The few negative reviews pointed out its sometimes rambling narration and burdensome legal history

(Gold 6), the positive ones praised its power, drama, and lack of sentimentality (Walton 7). Nevertheless, for some reason that only a market expert could tell, the book was not a big seller. It went through only one printing of about 2,500 copies, a relatively modest number (Brooks, "To Brainard Cheney" 20 Feb.), even for 1939, and it was serialized, in a condensed version, in the November, December, and January issues of *Scribner's Commentator.*

Frances (Fanny) Cheney looks on proudly as her husband signs copies of *Lightwood*, his first novel, October, 1939, at Zibart's Bookstore in Nashville. (*Courtesy Vanderbilt University Special Collections*)

In their November issue, the editors of the *Commentator* announced it as their major feature—"an exciting new novel about the wilds of Georgia, after the Civil War! A story of full-blooded, fighting, living people—A piece of life lifted from America's incredible past" (Cheney, "*Lightwood* (condensed)"). Perhaps the sale of *Lightwood* would have been larger if Houghton-Mifflin had not agreed to this serialization, the subscribers to the *Commentator* having no need to buy a copy of a book they had already read in their magazine.

Although he had hoped the book would sell better, Cheney was nevertheless pleased by the reception of *Lightwood*. He felt that he had told a significant story, that the public had enjoyed it, and that the critics had received it as serious fiction, written on a professional level.

CHAPTER V

River Rogue

A Novel of the Rise and Fall
of a Timber Baron

While contemplating the reception of *Lightwood*, Cheney had been turning over in his mind an idea for his next novel. His new idea was to write a story about the rivermen of southeast Georgia. He had many rich experiences of the river from which to draw. Rivers had always fascinated him in his youth, and he had recently returned from a remarkable adventure on the rivers of Tennessee that he had undertaken for the *Nashville Banner*.

Cheney had grown up near the confluence of three of southeast Georgia's most important rivers—the Altamaha, Oconee, and Ocmulgee. As a boy, he had fished the rivers with Robin Bess, swum in them with his friends, and listened to the river stories of the old-timers who used to raft timber down to Darien, Georgia. When he was nineteen, he had taken a raft trip down the river himself, as a sub-bow hand and cook on a raft of three. That adventure stayed fresh on his mind over the years. "On that memorable first trip we had tied up our rafts for the first night's camp at Gray's landing. . .our meal of fatback, blackeyed peas, sweet potatoes, cornpone, and coffee seemed sumptuous there before the blaze, the rain outside still falling. And afterward we lay back on our blankets and listened to Tobe's [the pilot's] tall tales. And I thought what a fine thing rafting could be as I fell off into a bottomless sleep" (Cheney, "Look-a, Look-a Yonder," 162-163).

The fascination of a river, its movement and mysteries, remained through the years an important part of Cheney's psyche, of his imagination. A year before he left the *Banner,* he dreamed up the adventurous idea of retracing the river voyage of Colonel John Donelson, the founder of the city of Nashville. He sold the idea to his editor and the U.S. Corps of Engineers. On April 13, 1939, he and two other men, Captain Paul Underwood and John Linder of the Corps of Engineers, set forth on a one thousand mile river voyage from Ft. Patrick Henry (now Kingsport, Tennessee) on the Holston River to Big French Lick

(Nashville) on the Cumberland. They called their seventeen-foot dual engine skiff the Adventure II, after Colonel Donelson's flatboat, the Adventure ("Cheney Ready to Start").

Author Brainard Cheney photographed in 1941 along the Altamaha River in Georgia while researching his novel *River Rogue*.

The Corps of Engineers co-sponsored the trip to improve its public relations and to conduct surveys of the three connecting rivers, the Holston, the Tennessee, and the Cumberland. The *Banner* was interested in featuring a series on the voyage that Cheney would send in as he traveled down the river.

This turned out to be a good idea. Cheney gathered information about the historic sites on the river, and he read a copy of Colonel Donelson's diary, "Voyage of the Donelson Party—1779." From these sources and his daily experiences of the Adventure II, he created informative and dramatic accounts of the ways of the river and the hardships of pioneer life. The *Banner* gave front-page space to several of the articles in the series, and each town along the river had a special write-up of the voyage in its own local newspaper.

Cheney wrote of the "bitter hardship and travail that beset the pioneers who were largely women and children. Their flatboats stuck on the shoals of the Holston. They suffered frostbite. From the present site of Chattanooga, Indians badgered them along their way to muscle Shoals, captured and killed twenty-eight smallpox victims aboard a pest boat" (*Adventure II*).

The Adventure II had its own turn with tragedy. On April 8, just five days after departure, a fire broke out on the boat near the gasoline-powered motors. "It blazed up suddenly, enveloping [John] Linder, causing him to dive overboard. 'We were powerless to aid Johnny in the river' said Cheney, 'for we could not regain control of the blazing boat until we crashed into the bank. . . We were unconvinced that he had drowned until after our fruitless search and discovery of his burned life preserver afloat told us'" ("Fire on Motor Boat"). Linder's body was found after a day of dragging the river. He had died by flame inhalation rather than drowning. Cheney wanted to call off the trip, but the Corps of Engineers and the *Banner* encouraged him to continue. Another engine operator from the Corps joined them to complete the voyage.

Three weeks and one thousand miles of river later, they made port in Nashville on April 24, the 160th anniversary of the landing of Donelson's party. They were met in Nashville with celebration and fanfare from city officials, representatives of the Corps of Engineers, and reporters from the *Banner*.

In his last article about the trip Cheney wrote:

We of Adventure II have retraced that course and have tried to view it in its historic significance along the way. . . and for the crew of Adventure II it is a pleasant ending, too. It was for us the retelling of a great yarn, and for us, too, a memorable voyage. It mixed the grisly and harsh with much that was enjoyable and pleasant. I will not live long enough to forget Johnnie Linder, ablaze from gasoline fire, leaping over my shoulder into the Tennessee from our skiff. . . .But there was the morning of April sun, when we started down the sparkling stairway of shoals at Poor Valley in the Holston, with its mountain furbishing of green and redbud. And that fried chicken supper we ate at Florence after a full day of wallowing in the windy waves of Wheeler and Wilson lakes. There was the 104-mile grind from Perryville to Birmingham (Kentucky) in wind and rain and there was the summer sun over the lake at Decatur, where the mud turtles warmed on the logs. . . .With a thousand miles of varied river, weather and fortune behind us, the crew of Adventure II today concludes a memorable voyage ("21-Day Voyage Traces Course").

A few months after Cheney left the *Banner* in 1940, he received a fellowship to Middlebury College's Bread Loaf Writers Conference in Vermont. The conference lasted two weeks, and it gave him the chance to meet and get to know several other American writers, such as Carson McCullers, Eudora Welty, John Ciardi, and Louis Untermeyer. The fellows were free to attend seminars, to socialize, or to use the time writing. During his stay, Cheney began outlining his idea for *River Rogue,* his new novel about the rivermen of Georgia.

Cheney attended the Breadloaf Writers Conference in 1941, here pictured with fellow attendees. Seated left to right: Edna Fredrickson, director Theodore Morrison, and Carson McCullers. Standing left to right: Eudora Welty, John Ciardi, Brainard Cheney, Marion Sims and Louis Untermeyer. *(Courtesy Vanderbilt University Special Collections)*

Even though his Adventure II experience was still fresh in his mind, he decided to return to Georgia after the conference to gather more material. "I decided last summer that I must ride a raft again, before I began writing my story of the raftsman's stubborn struggle with the river. For months, I had been digging into rivermen's recollections of the days of timber traffic. Up and down the Oconee, the Ocmulgee, the Altamaha I had tracked down old men, white and African American, who sat on their porches, warming rheumatic joints in the sun, or in shuttered shanties, shading glare-blinded eyes. We had swapped tobacco, taken drinks together and tried to recapture some part of that whopping adventure. And we did, much of it through the prysmic light of memory. But I felt a need of testing that vision with my senses" (Cheney, "Travel Deluxe" 14).

He found a raft of ash wood and a crew that agreed to take him on the one-hundred-mile trip to a lumber mill downriver. Finding such a crew was a stroke of luck because rafting timber was a long forgotten way of the river. The wood that made up its raft had been cut from land too far away from the road for the logging trucks. The trip gave him a chance to rekindle the memory of his boyhood days and the stories of the river that were told to him in his youth.

With the help of a Guggenheim Fellowship ($120 per month for twelve months), he was able to work the entire next year on *River Rogue*. Toward the end of his writing, he went to Darien, Georgia, the major setting of his novel, to write. He finished the last chapter on December 7, 1941. "When the echoes of Pearl Harbor destroyed our reposeful Sunday air last December they jolted me into the importunate present from the security of those bland Victorian years of the country's turn. To be sure, they jolted everybody else, but I trust not so far, or so rudely. I was, physically, in Darien, a Darien tranquil enough, but, laboring with the final chapters of *River Rogue*, I was encompassed by a scene a half-century more remote in morals, in hopes and in a sense of security. Of course I had seen the storm approaching many months before, but I had turned my eyes inward and, out of a sense of necessity, barricaded myself behind fictional walls of my own creation" (Cheney, "See Here, Private Cheney" 8). The war later changed the current of his life away from fiction, but for a few months after the bombing of Pearl Harbor, he was engaged in reworking *River Rogue* and trying to get it published.

In *River Rogue*, Cheney returns to his subject of the failing hero. Like Micajah Corn, Ratliff Sutton, the protagonist in *River Rogue*, engages in a long heroic struggle that ends in defeat. Unlike Micajah, however, Ratliff does not possess at the beginning of the story all the heroic qualities of character necessary for the struggle. Instead, he is a strange, insecure boy of fifteen who lives in 1884 with an African American family in the swamps of South Georgia.

At the impressionable age of eleven, Ratliff had discovered that his mother, a few months after his father's death, had taken up with several men from the town. When she gave birth to an illegitimate child, a sense of betrayal, shame, and public disgrace cut deep into his mind. Cheney dramatizes this young boy's "coming into knowledge" in a short scene—an epiphany— between Ratliff and a townsman.

> Mace Rawlins was looking at him from the main street of Nine-and-a-Quarter: "What yuh gonna call this heah kid of yuh ma's? What's his last name? Looks like yore pa's lease done run out befoh this un come."
>
> Again he sensed that first confusion in believing that he had not heard Mace right. The man had never spoken to him before. Then he knew for a second time the feeling that his clothes had suddenly been jerked off him . . .The suspicion about his mother he had not even admitted to himself was true, and the whole town was talking about it.
>
> Then there came that flow of unreal fire from outside him that moved through his whole body, lifted him like a burning piece of paper, and his seeing, in the flash of it, that he must kill his mother, his bastard brother, that he must kill the man who did this to them, that he must kill Mace Rawlins. It had been only a moment, then he was a floating cinder; everything had gone blank. (Cheney, *River Rogue* 26)

Ratliff does not kill anyone; instead, he runs away from the family and the society that has made him feel shameful and contemptible. For days, he wanders blindly in the wilderness and swamps near the Ocmulgee River. Uncle Mundy Sutton, an elderly African American man who had known his father, finds him and allows Ratliff to stay with him and his family. Ratliff feels secure in this remote home, at the very bottom of the social ladder, far from the sneers of his own race. To disavow his personal history, he changes his name from Flournoy to that of his African American friends and becomes known as Ratliff (sometimes Rattler or Snake) Sutton.

The event of Ratliff's public disgrace looms as large in his mind as the humiliation of another youth, with a similar name, in a different novel. In Faulkner's *Absalom Absalom!* Thomas Sutpen's tragic fate is forged by a similar incident, an intractable moment of shame on the front porch of a Southern plantation.

And now he [the 13-year-old Sutpen] stood there before that white door with the monkey nigger barring it and looking down at him in his patched made-over jeans clothes and no shoes, and I don't reckon he had even ever experimented with a comb because that would be one of the things that his sisters would keep hidden good. He had never thought about his own hair or clothes or anybody else's hair or clothes until he saw that monkey nigger, who through no doing of his own happened to have had the felicity of being housebred in Richmond maybe, looking—("Or maybe even in Charleston," Shreve breathed.)—at them and he never even remembered what the nigger said, how it was the nigger told him, even before he had had time to say what he came for, never to come to that front door again but to go around to the back. (Faulkner 232)

Like Faulkner's character, Ratliff spends his life trying to regain his lost sense of social respect and self-esteem. His struggle, too, becomes compulsive and blinding, ending in tragedy.

Ratliff's climb to power provides the basic structure of *River Rogue*. He begins his struggle as a raftsman on the rivers of South Georgia and ends it as a wealthy and respectable member of society. Each incident in the novel either lifts him toward success and self-respect or throws him backward, down toward ignominy and disgrace.

Cheney divides *River Rogue* into three sections: Poss, China, and Robbie. The Poss section portrays Ratliff's slow rise to power on the river. Ratliff's first ambition is to become a successful raftsman, yet the river, as Uncle Mundy says, is a "hard teacher." His first failure comes when he and Poss Sutton, a young relative of Uncle Mundy's, float a timber raft down the Oconee and Altamaha rivers to a lumber mill at Darien, Georgia. Coming into Darien, Ratliff is excited and happy. This adventure is his first step into the social world since he left his family four years earlier. His joy, however, is suddenly deflated by a rough and unscrupulous raftsman who halts them at the dock with an accusation of theft:

The man was studying the logs again. He turned to the inspector. "That's my raft—most of it. Those hewn logs: I'd know Nigger Ned's work anywhere." He spat into the water. "Couple of green, no-'count raft hands run off and left it up at Hard Bargain."

Ratliff had had a cold feeling in his marrow ever since the men approached and he hadn't known where to begin to defend himself. Now his lower lip tightened. Hard Bargain! Hard Bargain was on the Ocmulgee; their logs had come off the Oconee, most of them. The fellow's bluffing, they thought.

"Those hewn timbers are mine, boy." The man looked back. "Where'd you git hold of 'em?". . . .

"Ain't naer stick of it you'n! This raft belongs to my uncle. Hard Bargain ain't never seen it. It come off'n the Oconee—at his place on Dead River. He didn't come along 'cause he's sick. I aim to sell it for 'im and take the money back to 'im. And I don't aim to be bothered." Ratliff resumed his slow backing away. "Not by you, naer nobody else!". . . .

He [the man] stopped, stuck his thumbs in his belt. "This uncle you're claimin' so big is an old swamp-rat nigger: Mundy Sutton. Hangs around Dead River, fishin' and stealin' people's hogs. And you are the white-trash, renegade boy that lives with 'im—lives theah in the swamp with niggers, in the house with niggers—in the bed with 'em, too, I reckon."

He gripped his belt harshly. "You're nuthin' but a white nigger—livin' with nigger swamp rats that never had a stick of timber they didn't steal in their lives. You kain't name yore pappy, naer yore mammy, and you're just the same as a nigger." (Cheney, *River Rogue* 22-23)

After the disgrace of being slandered and having his raft taken from him, Ratliff returns to Uncle Mundy's sickened by defeat. He stays in his room for days, hidden within himself. When he comes out, he takes to the work of the farm in stoic, mute silence, hardly speaking with anyone for months.

Nearly a year after his defeat in Darien, he has the good fortune of working for Bud True, a respected and expert raftsman. Over long months of apprenticeship, Ratliff finally gains the respect of the rivermen. He is quick, intelligent, and courageous, and under Bud's direction, he learns the ways of the river and the codes of the raftsmen. However, Ratliff later becomes restless. Bud's ways are often too slow, too conservative; he is not quick to take advantage of situations. Eventually, Ratliff leaves the tutelage of Bud True to set out rafting timber on his own.

One of the implied rules in Cheney's world of the novel is that any man can raise himself from the depths to the height of society by cunning, intelligence, and will. But he must not break any of the other rules of life in the process. He must not exploit his fellow man; he must not be in too big a hurry to succeed; and he must not become proud, "too big for his britches." For if he does, that great force behind the universe—be it Fate or God or Nature—will humble him.

Ratliff suffers several such disciplinary actions in *River Rogue*. They usually occur after he experiences a success that puffs up his pride and distorts his judgment. When he makes an error, Nature corrects him with a devastating blow. Once in his haste to get a raft of timber to market, Ratliff decides to begin the voyage at night, without regard for the advice of Uncle Mundy.

How, in the name of common sense, did Uncle Mundy think they'd ever get off tonight without everybody helping some? he said. Tonight! In this freshet? Uncle

Mundy caught hold of the sides of the boat and crawled out. He straightened up before he spoke again. "You talk lak you ain't got much respeck for dis river, not like no raftsman!"

Ratliff frowned and jerked up his chin. "Do? Well, I got respeck enough to know if we don't go pretty quick, we may not be able to in another week." He went on to say that then everybody between Dublin and Darien would be floating ash out of the swamps and drifting it down the river to put a freshet on the market.

"Dat's a thing yuh got to git used to if'n you run de river," Uncle Mundy said.

Sure, if you trifled around and let it happen, Ratliff told him. Uncle Mundy spoke to Poss, too; he urged them both to stop and come on to the house, but when Ratliff said angrily that he would eat supper in Darien three nights hence, he went back to his boat. He stopped beside it and turned again. He looked gaunt and bent in the firelight, but he brought his shoulders up straight. "Dis river a big man! You act like you don't know dat." (Cheney, *River Rogue* 117)

The trip ends in disaster and death. In the middle of the night, their raft runs ashore on one of the river's treacherous bends:

The oar jumped out of his [Ratliff's] hands, caught on a tree-trunk. Its blade bent like a hoop and snapped. There were more trees; crunching, crackling noise. The butting binder jumped into the air. Logs reared up. He felt himself going upward, and leaped.

Warm, thick water closed over him, piled on top. He was rushed along, bumping into things. He tried to pull up to the surface and his head hit a log. He pushed downward and was swept on. He bumped a tree, caught it, and was swung around to the lower side. He made the surface and held to the trunk, panting. He could not see anything, but he could still hear limbs crackling and breaking. Gone to hell! he thought—the whole caboodle!

He got his wind and yelled, "Where yuh, Poss?" He could hear his echo above the rattling current. He called again. It brought only an echo. "Goddamnit, Poss! Answer me!" He kept yelling. (Cheney, *River Rogue* 123)

In the China section, Cheney takes his hero through a new series of successes and failures. Ratliff's achievements include becoming the lover and confidant of China Swann, the beautiful and prosperous madam of Darien's most prestigious brothel; saving the life of Bud True, which regains for him the respect of the raftsmen, respect that he had lost because of Poss' death; creating a new kind of raft oar, "Sutton's lazypin," that improves rafting; and outwitting the rich lumber companies by selling them "doctored," defective logs. These successes, however, do not satisfy Ratliff's ambition.

When the lumber market fails in the Panic of 1893 and the price of timber goes down, Ratliff comes to see that the raftsmen are only pawns of the timber companies. He feels an almost ordained need to help them; unconsciously, he identifies his personal sense of being wronged by life with the cause of the exploited raftsmen. He tries to convince them to voluntarily hold back their timber to drive up its market price. When this fails, he calls a meeting of raftsmen and tries to get them to join in a confederacy to create an embargo of timber on the river:

He halted and gazed around the semicircle rapidly. "There's thirty-six of us and fourteen rafts; that's plenty." He wheeled about, looking out across the river. "She ain't more'n a hundred and fifty paces wide here and well banked. Three-four rafts tied together will boom 'er." He faced the men. "And that's what I aim for us to do; boom 'er, and not let another raft git by to Darien!". . . .

"Jesus Christ, I thought you were goan have a plan to bust up the companies, aer at least trick 'em!" Bostick said. "Not git into a fight with raftsmen!" He turned away without looking at Ratliff and followed Haynes.

The men in the circle stared at Ratliff now. Their necks were stiff, their faces hard.

"Hell, we couldn't tell them fellers they kain't take theah rafts to Darien," said a glass-eyed fat man, tightening his belt. "That don't make sense!"

"My pappy's aimin' to bring a big cypress raft down about the last of the month—I kin see myself standin' theah telling him he kain't git by!" said Boze Wall. He tried a laugh that rose shrilly and broke. "He'd scorch my tail with a Winchester!" (Cheney, *River Rogue* 289, 292)

Ratliff's failure to be elected as the raftsmen's leader both humiliates and angers him. He doesn't understand that whereas he is willing to use any means to accomplish his goal, they are not. He interprets their loyalty to other raftsmen as ignorance, a failure to comprehend the larger picture that he sees. Feeling rejected and defeated, Ratliff breaks his bonds with the raftsmen and turns his back on a way of life that had brought him respect and a sense of belonging.

In the second half of *River Rogue*, Cheney introduces a new class of society. Before, the reader knows only of poor farmers, raftsmen, saloons and bawdy houses; now he discovers that Darien, which is the central timber market in the region, also has a genteel society. The timber barons, lumber mill owners, and merchants of the town have a separate existence from the raftsmen—one that includes a more elegant way of life, with colonial homes, balls, churches, and city councils.

After Ratliff quits the river and the problems of the raftsmen, the conquest of Darien's aristocracy becomes the new goal

of his unrelenting need for power and respect. Cheney struc-
tures this new struggle for acceptance, like Ratliff's earlier one,
in a rhythmical series of success and failure. Just as Cheney
had Ratliff begin his struggle on the river with the humiliation
of having his first raft taken from him, so he has him start this
second battle from a position of failure and disgrace.

After working for a couple of years in a Darien tavern as a
joint owner with China Swann, Ratliff applies for the job of
public timber scaler, a public position that requires a vote of
confidence from the town council. Although he rallies a little
support for his appointment from the African American community of Darien, the city council turns him down with contempt.

> "I confess I cannot appreciate Councilman Jaeger's
> viewpoint, but I wonder if he knows, and if you, Major Mac-
> gregor, and the other councilmen here, know that R. P. Sut-
> ton, in the timber trade, goes by the fitting sobriquet of
> 'Snake'—and that he is the same Snake Sutton who was in-
> dicted some years ago by a McIntosh County Grand Jury for
> doctoring his logs?". . .
>
> Possibly some of the members had even heard of one by
> the name of Swann, called China. He had been reliably in-
> formed that this individual was the *fille de joie* of this appli-
> cant for high public office. He must perforce be even blunt-

er with his fellow councilmen: *fille de joie* was scarcely the word—kept woman. And that was wide of the mark still. It appeared that the woman was doing the keeping! . . .

"I am confident that the colored citizens of Darien have been deceived in the character of the man who has been foisted upon them, for their support." His eyes fastened on Caldwell. "I say, I am confident that they would not knowingly support a criminal, an ex-outlaw and a fugitive from justice, a whoremonger and a procurer!" (Cheney, *River Rogue* 309-310)

Ratliff leaves the council, enraged and disgraced. Remembering his first humiliation when he learned of his mother's debauchery, he instinctively feels like running away from society. China Swann, who is as important a mentor for Ratliff in this struggle as Bud True was in the earlier one, explains to him that life in town follows a different set of rules than life on the river.

"The rules are different here, so are the things that count. You were the best shot and axeman on the river, but that ain't worth a dime here. You were the slickest of the timber-runners, but you can't slide on that in Darien. You settled your differences with a maul or a gun on the river, but that don't go a peg in Darien—won't get you anywhere, except the jailhouse. You've got to put those councilmen's names down in your books and bide your time till you are ready to pay 'em off—and first, you've got to catch on to their tricks, not get caught, not be a sucker for 'em.". . .

"You've got to beat 'em at their own game to make 'em swallow their words—to make 'em afraid of you and respect you. Money is the only thing that makes a man talk, or hold his tongue, in this town." Panting, and relaxing her hold, she felt near enough to the truth. She went on: "Those bastards don't even see they were low-ratin' you; you are just a penniless nobody to them. If you had been Mr. Ten Thousand Dollars, instead of Pocket Change, why you'd have met with bowing and scraping. You wouldn't have known yourself, the way they'd have spread it on." (Cheney, *River Rogue* 315-316)

In the last third of the novel, the *Robbie* section, Ratliff slowly climbs the ladder of Darien society—from tavern keeper to gambling house owner and timber inspector for one of the largest timber companies to the public scaler position from which he had earlier been rejected. His climb is slow but methodical, acquiring at each step more money and more power for himself.

He eventually marries Robbie MacGregor, the daughter of one of the most powerful timber buyers in Darien. Consistent with the structural pattern of the novel, this success leads to a greater failure. When Ratliff and his wife return from their wedding trip to New Orleans, they find that Robbie's father, who violently disapproved of Ratliff and the marriage, had suffered a stroke. The town's aristocracy, in sympathy with the father, punish the ungrateful daughter and her upstart husband with social ostracism. This deepest rebuke enflames Ratliff's last and greatest effort. He resolves to defeat the timber barons and force Darien's aristocracy into submission.

Ratliff gains the initiative in this contest through an act of nature. In 1898, a hurricane hits the coast and tidewater regions of south Georgia, wrecking the coastal and river towns, sweeping more than forty million feet of company timber away from the boons, wharves, and mills out into the surrounding rivers and marshes. Ratliff, quick to seize an advantage, turns this public disaster into a private fortune. He hurriedly organizes teams of raftsmen to recover the lost timber. While others are trying to rebuild the town, he is out on the river from dawn to dusk gathering his stockpiles of timber. Later, he sets up his own mill and begins selling lumber while the other companies are deadlocked in lawsuits—claims and counter-claims of theft—against each other. As he becomes the most prosperous and solvent of the timber barons, the society that was once closed to him and his wife receives him with open arms and obsequious smiles. His triumph, however, is short-lived.

At the height of his victory over Darien society, one of Robbie's most disapproving relatives drops her censure of the marriage. When Ratliff learns that she seeks reconciliation, he breaks out in unguarded, fiendish laughter that betrays his hardness to both himself and his wife:

"She came to me after the services—she wants us to have a talk together."

"Who?" he said, his gaze still on the blaze.

"Aunt Mag."

He gripped the mantel. Aunt Mag! Her image—the cold mouth crumpling, the stiff neck bent—flashed before him. His face slowly flushed, as if with drink, and suddenly he was laughing—quietly, evenly at first, as a hen cackles, then harsh and high.

"Ratliff!" Robbie cried out.

He looked up, his jaw caught back, and saw her staring at him. She had recoiled; her lips were parted, the gathering flesh at her cheekbones trembled, her eyes were wide and dark. Quickly, she turned and hurried from the room.

Ratliff!—the sound echoed back from the shut door, like a whiplash—Ratliff! The first passion he had seen on her face since her father's death—and it was fear, cold fear! What in God's name had he done? He grew weak and sick. It was as if he'd struck her! "You clumsy fool!" he said aloud. But why was she so frightened? They'd licked the Dales—brought Aunt Mag around. But he could not dismiss the memory of her eyes. They stared at him, as if they were seeing him for the first time, as if he were hideous! (Cheney, *River Rogue* 407-408)

Ratliff's victory over Darien society is further spoiled by the sudden death of his wife. Away in Philadelphia on a financial venture, he receives the incredible news that Bud True, his oldest friend, has, in a drunken rage, killed his wife. This complication of forces so near the end of the novel confuses more than enriches Cheney's denouement. The reader looks unsuccessfully for credible reasons for such an unexpected turn of events. Cheney renders a believable murder scene between Bud True and Robbie—she had been bringing food and clothing to Bud's sick wife, with Bud feeling humiliated and impotent by the charity and finally striking her in a blind, drunken rage. However, the more important relationship between Bud and Ratliff, which was so well presented earlier in the novel, is developed with less satisfaction.

Ratliff had exploited Bud in a number of his ventures over the years: using him, after Bud had received a disabling accident on the river, as a bar keeper, inspector, and co-owner (in name only) of his lumber mill. Ratliff had later demoted him because of his excessive drinking, from inspector to night watchman. Bud could not stand what had happened to him over the years. He had gone from respectable raftsman to town drunk. Although Ratliff's fate had been the opposite—from raftsman to timber baron—his integrity, once he left the river, had gone downward like Bud's fortune.

Cheney does not, however, establish clearly how these two actions are linked. Bud's corruption comes more from bad luck and intemperance than from his relationship with Ratliff. If Cheney could have established a stronger causal relationship between Bud's fall and Ratliff's ascendancy, Bud would have become for the reader a symbol of Ratliff's lost integrity and, therefore, a perfect instrument to administer Fate's deathly blow to the proud and successful Ratliff.

Cheney has Fate strike this blow against Ratliff because as an heroic figure, Ratliff, like Micajah Corn in *Lightwood*, is found to be insufficient. Even though his struggle for social approval and self-respect gives birth to heroic qualities of intelligence, shrewdness, courage, and will, the struggle becomes so compelling that it blots out his humanness. Driven by an unrelenting need for power and respect, he becomes hard, proud, and self-centered, forsaking old friends and using any means to gain his objective. By his acts, he becomes a stranger to the human community for which he so desperately sought. In Cheney's world of the novel, a character who loses his human-ness is inadequate to meet the challenge of life; he must, there-fore, ultimately fail, even though his efforts to prevail be of he-roic dimensions.

At the end of the novel, Ratliff comes to see what the strug-gle has done to him and why he has failed. In a moment of recognition, he reflects about his fate.

"Power is not enough!" he said finally and aloud, "here or anywhere." The horse moved slowly on. You called them [the raftsmen] blind, butt-headed bastards there on Clayhole Bluff, he told himself. You quit the river and came to town. But you never did join up—to anything. Yes, you thought you'd joined with Robbie, but you never did accept her—what she stood for. You tried to make her yours; what you stood for.

And what was that? Nothing. Nothing, but your selfish-ness! It had been something once, but you kicked it off be-hind you. You had no crowd. You had no rules—you dropped them, too, after you got here; you broke your bonds with everyone—and self, blind self, swallowed you (Cheney, *River Rogue* 441).

Victorious, but defeated, having won every battle on the riv-ers and in the towns, yet losing everyone that he cared for, Ratliff gives up the struggle. He tells his lawyers that he will not press charges against his old friend, Bud True, and he leaves town—headed back to the river, back to a new beginning free from ambition and pride.

Houghton Mifflin published *River Rogue* in 1942, and it was well received by the critics. In an article for the *Saturday Review of Literature,* Robert Penn Warren said,

> This second novel by Brainard Cheney is a solid, inter-esting, and at times exciting book and marks a decided ad-vance over his *Lightwood.* . . .The world of the novel is the world of the rivers down which the raftsmen brought their timber to the Darien market in the last years of the past century. The quality of the world—the aspect of the country, and the details of the occupation, the sprees in the bars and dives of Darien, the cunning, viciousness, and honor of the rogues, the code of the raftsmen, who felt themselves set apart from other men—is rendered with a fine imaginative precision ("East Georgia" 25).

Even the negative reviews found favorable things to say about it.

> A book which puts Brainard Cheney high among the strictly regional novelists—a book so good (when it is) that its weaknesses are doubly deplorable. . .Brainard Cheney

writes with the homely hardness of a grindstone. At his best
he is a master at making detail, action and physical sensa-
tion palpable, and almost Homerically fresh. At his worst he
is a pedestrian writer, capable of serious lapses of literary
judgment, but enormously sensitive to a certain landscape
and a certain people. If he ever wrestles a subject his size
with grace as well as grit, he may make literary history
(Cheney, *Time* 94).

Donald Davidson wrote a perceptive review of the novel
for the *Sewanee Review*. He pointed out that as Cheney
took his hero, Snake Sutton, further away from his original
conception of him and further away from Sutton's early life
in the river, the plot and character weaken, but that "Mr.
Cheney's gifts are decidedly at their best when he presents
rugged and unwashed characters in bold action out of
doors. All the rafting scenes, all the episodes that engage
Snake [Ratliff] in some hardship from which he can emerge
only by daring or muscle or native craft—all these are excellent, are beyond all criticism. They have the freshness that
comes from a new subject matter, a good story about a ro-
guish hero, plainly and directly told" (Davidson 165).

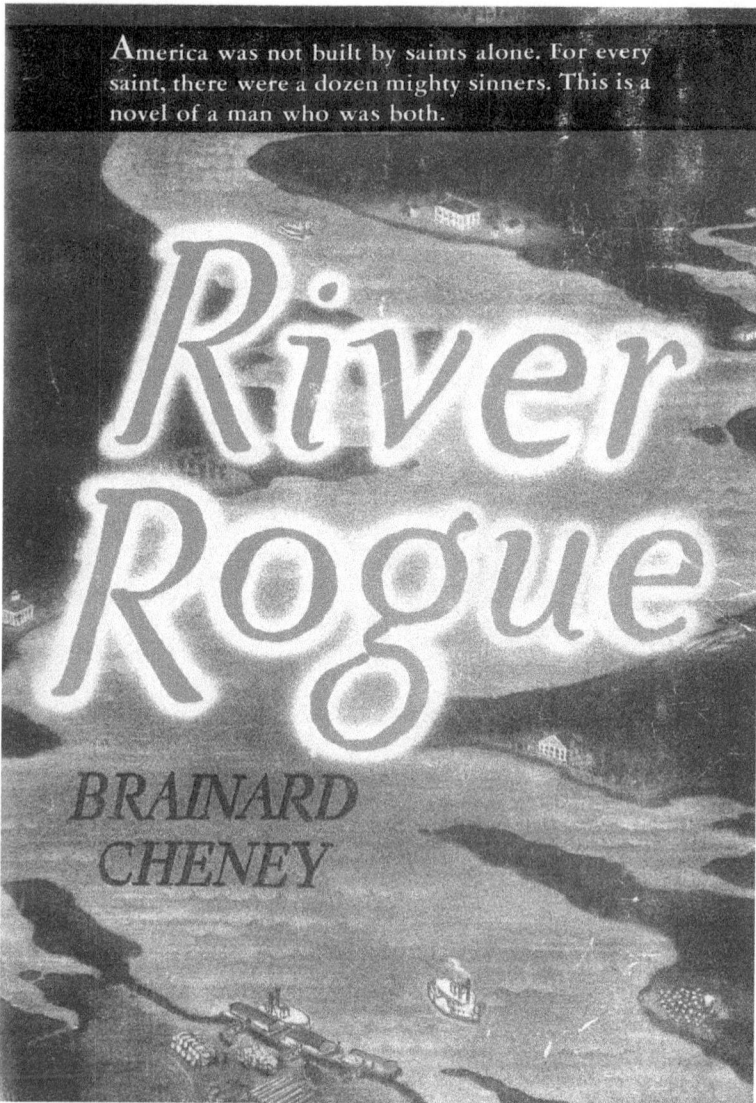

America was not built by saints alone. For every saint, there were a dozen mighty sinners. This is a novel of a man who was both.

River Rogue

BRAINARD CHENEY

River Rogue, Cheney's second novel, published by Houghton Mifflin in 1942, featured a fanciful cover depicting the Altamaha River basin and the port of Darien, Georgia in its heyday circa 1890s.

River Rogue sold much better than *Lightwood*. The initial printing was for 3,800 copies, and another 5,000 were sold by a second publisher, Grossett and Dunlap Company (Brooks, Letter to Brainard Cheney). Had it not been for one squeamish member of the board of editors of the Book of the Month Club, who objected to some of the rough scenes in the novel, *River Rogue* would have been chosen as the Book of the Month Club's featured selection, an act that would have ensured the selling of thousands of more copies (Cheney, Letter to Paul Brooks).

Cheney's career, though successful and impressive, was sprinkled with "near hits." *River Rogue* even had a brush with Hollywood. Metro-Goldwyn-Mayer was interested in making a film version of it. They bought an option on the book from Cheney but gave up on the project at the last moment when they realized that the cost of production was going to go beyond their wartime budget (Fadiman, Letter to Nannine Joseph).

Cheney was not very disappointed by these "near hits" because in *River Rogue*, he had created an interesting story that had also captured an era of the nation's history, a way of life that had vanished from the American scene. All the stories that he had been told about the rivers of Georgia and the raftsmen had been made to live again and had been preserved for the future in his fiction. In addition, the public and critics had enjoyed his book, and he now had more pressing things on his mind. The United States had finally entered the Second World War, and Cheney, having missed WWI as a young cadet at The Citadel, was determined to serve his country.

CHAPTER VI
The Battle for Washington

For months after the bombing of Pearl Harbor, Cheney tried to enter military service. Even though he was forty-one years old, he felt healthy, active, and equal to the physical demands of military training. However, he was turned down by every branch of the service—Marines, Army, Navy, and Air Force. His last hope—to be drafted by his local board—was thwarted when the federal government passed a law prohibiting the induction of men over forty. In order to serve his country, though in a less direct manner than he preferred, Cheney accepted a position as advisor and secretary to Tennessee's United States Senator, Tom Stewart. In a Western Union telegram to Stewart, Cheney wrote, "Stymied on military service. Glad to take that job if still open." This appointment, at least, brought him to the nation's capitol where the major decisions of the war were being made.

In December of 1942, Cheney left Tennessee to fight the "Battle of Washington" (Cheney, Telegram to Senator Tom Stewart).

Tom Stewart had already served one unimpressive term in the Senate when he was counseled by his friends to find a political advisor who could help him gain public and congressional recognition. During the next three years, Cheney succeeded in promoting Stewart. He spent weeks researching and documenting the speeches that Stewart delivered in the Senate, speeches that Cheney thinks helped pave the way to Stewart's appointment to the chairmanship of the Senate's Committee on Small Businesses in America. From this position Stewart acquired the power and esteem that he wanted (Cheney, Interview 4 April).

Although Cheney had little time for literary enterprises during his Washington years, he was able to continue an association with many of the country's leading writers. In September 1943 Allen Tate received a one-year appointment to the post of Consultant in Poetry to the Library of Congress (Squires and Tate 174-175).

It was difficult for the Tates to find a suitable home in wartime Washington. When Caroline finally found a house she liked she named it the "Bird Cage" after the 'fancy' house in Cheney's novel, *River Rogue*.

The Cheneys shared a house with married couple Allen Tate and Caroline Gordon during their Washington years. *(Courtesy Princeton University Library, Department of Rare Books and Special Collections)*

Knowing that the Cheneys were in Washington, Tate secured a position for Mrs. Cheney as his assistant in the Library of Congress; working together that year, they compiled the bibliography, *Sixty American Poets, 1896-1944* (Library of Congress, 1945). Later in her life, Mrs. Cheney received an Honorary Doctor of Letters from Marquette University and many other prestigious awards for her long service and contributions to the field of Library Science.

To reduce the expenses of Washington housing, the Cheneys and Tates shared a two-story house near the Capitol. This home became a frequent meeting place for such distinguished writers as John Peale Bishop, Archibald MacLeish, and Katherine Ann Porter; it also served as a place to visit while in Washington for the Cheneys' and Tates' literary friends from Tennessee.

During these years from 1942 to 1945, Cheney's political perspective widened significantly. His old dream—to overcome the limitations of his youth and to participate in the larger world outside of rural Georgia—had finally come to pass. From his position in the nation's Capitol, he saw the political and military drama of the war on the national and worldwide scale, and his understanding of world events became considerably sophisticated. In a letter advising Stewart against an attitude of

post-war isolationism, one can observe Cheney's skill of diplomacy as Stewart's advisor and his understanding of world politics:

You mentioned, in our conversation, prospective, at
least prospective at the time, congressional appropriations
for loans to the British, French, etc. you were asking the
question, "With a three-hundred-billion-dollar national
debt, how much more can we stand and what about future
domestic need for appropriations for public works?"

I don't know whether our Government should, or should
not make these foreign loans, to be sure. However, there are
a few things I would like to remind you about—even though
you have already considered them.

One: there is no longer any choice about isolationism—
we are up to our *a--* in international politics, whether we
like it or not. I know you know that, but I also know of the
loathing (I guess that word fits as well as any) with which
you regard the prospect of being mixed up in 'em. Just for
the good of your own soul, you ought to repeat to yourself
every day that isolationism is gone. It's a fact: there is no
more county politics, no more backyard economics. There is
no major domestic issue that may now come up, but that it
must be considered if it is wisely considered in the light of
international politics.

Of course, the British are in competition with us for foreign markets and the French would be too, if they could—
and we must not overlook that, but they are at the present
moment our chessmen in the big ring, the real politico-

economic competition, with Russia. It is at the moment apparently more political than economic, but it will become economic, as you know.

I am not so much alarmed about the ideological side of the USSR—I don't know what communism means to them, though I am sure it is not the same breed of politico-economic philosophy that Karl Marx devised, and I am reasonably certain that it is not the theoretical communism that most of the communist groups in the various West European countries think they are practicing. But it is a very effective international revolutionary propaganda, and the Russians command it effectively and realistically—not for the sake of any class creed, but for the advancement of Russia, an Asiatic, military dictatorship. And for protection, too, for the Soviets fear the Americans and the British (for even though they have gone socialist at home, they remain imperial in their foreign policy. Moreover, I doubt that Britain's socialism has any real kinship to whoever it is that obtains in Russia and that they call Communism).

The war is over and we are soon going to find out just how shaky is this world we are living in—God help us! (Cheney, "To Tom Stewart").

Cheney's analysis of the postwar economy and the impending split with the Soviet Union is impressive because it predates the coming Cold War Era by several years.

Although Cheney's intellectual horizons had broadened, his early liberal attitudes had substantially diminished. They had not withstood the test of experience. Since his days of political reporting on the *Nashville Banner* in the thirties until the end of his Washington years in 1946, his optimism about human nature and the prospects for social progress had slowly eroded away. The hard bargaining and often corrupt processes that he had first observed on a national level in the U.S. Senate destroyed his political idealism. He remembered that the hopes and dreams of Woodrow Wilson had not kept America out of war. Roosevelt's New Dealism had been brave and courageous, yet its implementation was often sabotaged at the local levels. The Second World War had assured Cheney that lasting peace was an illusion, and the advent of the Atomic Age had proven that reason had run mad in the world. In addition, his Utopian and socialistic beliefs fell apart when he realized that the Russian and Chinese experiments in social reform had turned into military dictatorships, suppressing the fundamental rights and liberties of the people they were supposed to be helping (Cheney, Interview 18 Feb.).

After leaving Washington, Cheney began his own campaign for the next six years to try to understand the problems of political idealism. Once again, as he had done in the twenties, he began asking the fundamental questions of life. What is the nature of man? Can social and political ideals be put into the service of humanity? What prevents the realization of ideals? Is man inherently good or evil? What is the best political system? Why do men of vision become degraded in the practice of politics? Is there direction and meaning to life? To find answers to these questions, Cheney began an educational process that joined a systematic reflection of his past with a program of extensive reading in religion, political science, history, philosophy, psychology, and anthropology. He read the works of Whitehead, Toynbee, Jung, and the French theologian, Teilhard de Chardin. He read Spengler's *Decline of the West*, Ortega y Gasset's The *Revolt of the Masses*, Northrup's *Meeting of East and West*, Arthur Eddington's *The Philosophy of Physical Science* and Erwin Schröedinger's *What is Life*_(Cheney, Interview 18 Feb.).

In talks with his Agrarian friends, Allen Tate, Andrew Lytle, and Donald Davidson, Cheney began to listen more earnestly to their conservative views about the nature of man and society. A good example of their powers of persuasion is a letter Davidson wrote to Cheney in 1948, defending the Agrarian concept of property.

The whole matter of property is very much misunder-
stood. I beseech you not to be tolled off into the Socialist
fallacy that "property is theft," and the Communist elabora-
tion of that error. I don't think there can be liberty—
personal or social—without private property, but I don't follow Locke altogether on the government-for-the-sake-of-
property conception. The Jefferson-Taylor of Carolina
ammendation, as further amended by our own Agrarians, is
what I hold to. I found out when I was in the Army what
happens when property belongs to the "government." How
anybody that's ever been in the Army can be friendly to socialism (much less Communism) is a great mystery to me?
People ought to learn from the Army (a highly "socialized"
device) that socialism can exert raw power for a limited objective—and that's all. It has no wisdom, no morals, no religion—except that, in the Army, but not in civil socialism,
the element of *actual* self-sacrifice supplies a code that substitutes for morals and religion, for a while, and a great haz-
ard.

I don't feel able to go into the metaphysics and episte-
mology of these matters. I was always weak in philosophy. I
do feel with all my soul that of all the delusions humanity
ever indulged in, socialism is the dullest, the stupidest, and
in the end the cruelest, most destructive and offensive (Davidson, "To Brainard Cheney").

The conservative attitude that men are self-serving and that
government is inherently corrupting was consistent with what
Cheney had learned from his political experiences. In an article

for the *International Encyclopedia of the Social Sciences*, Clinton Rossiter stated the proposition more bluntly that conservatism is the belief in "the obstinately imperfect nature of men, in which unreason and sinfulness lurk always behind the curtain of civilized behavior."

Yet the conservative view did not fill the emptiness created by the loss of his idealism. Skeptical, even cynical, about the possibilities of achieving social justice and general prosperity, Cheney could not altogether give up his feeling of hope about the future of man. This divided spirit left him with ambivalent feelings about the political process; he had learned that political idealism was a sentimental illusion, yet was there not something in life that could sustain a man's highest visions? And was there not some way that a statesman might remain unsullied by the political process?

In addition to talking with friends, thinking, and reading, Cheney decided to try to dramatize the issue of idealism vs. political reality in a novel. He hoped that this might help him see the problems more clearly and aid him in resolving his conflicting views. He was wrong. From 1945 to 1952, he wrote his political novel five times without satisfaction. The novel did not solve his philosophical dilemma; it only mirrored it.

The Image and the Cry

The Image and the Cry is the story of Bob Munson's personal and political life. It begins with Munson, ambitious, young, and idealistic, launching his political campaign for the governorship of a mid-south state. While out seeking votes among a group of farmers from a remote hill community in the state, he discovers that the farmers belong to a curious Pentecostal order called the Dolly Pond Church of God. They believe in proving their faith by bringing live, poisonous snakes into the church and by passing them around to the brethren who have become possessed by the spirit. Munson is intrigued by this bizarre religion, but being a modern man, he finds the practice irrational and insane. After attempting to secure their votes by assuring them that he believes in freedom of religion, he leaves the remote community, but he does not forget their mystifying ways of worship.

In the beginning of the campaign, Munson bases his appeal on a dream of equality and prosperity for all and on his opposition to the established Hawkins machine that runs the state government. However, when the leading newspaper unexpectedly drops its support of him, Munson realizes that he cannot win. He is approached by an old wartime friend, Fitzhugh Ball, a supporter of the Hawkins machine, who tries to persuade him into accepting the support of the organization. Munson wants the governorship too much to turn down the offer. He acquiesces and accepts their help. This becomes the first compromise in a long list that ends up four hundred pages later with the total disintegration of Munson's ideals and his personal life.

In Munson's long ride to destruction, Cheney depicts all the ins and outs of political action. The novel portrays strategy sessions in "smoke-filled rooms", cases of public posturing on issues that belie real attitudes, and examples of political infighting that show how the various alliances of power in a state shift about in self-serving manners. It portrays all the ways in which idealistic goals become tarnished in the process of swapping favors, compromising principals, qualifying beliefs, and employing illegal means to accomplish the public good.

When Munson becomes governor, he finds that he is obliged to reward the people of the Hawkins organization with favors of office and special considerations. The demands are endless. Besides having to accommodate the corruption of the machine that helped elect him, Munson realizes that even the great majority, "the people" that he fought for, is an illusion, a bodiless abstract, transformed into the political reality of individual lobbyist and pressure groups, fighting at cross purposes—all with their hands out. He manages to do some good while in office, but each political act degrades rather than uplifts him. He can get a minimum wage law passed, but only after dishonoring the last rites of a young, poverty-stricken woman who had committed suicide. He exploits the girl's tragedy by delivering a graveside speech against her employer, calculated to arouse public support for his bill.

Munson's private life is also corrupted by the political process. The Hawkins machine insists that he stay married to his estranged wife for the sake of his public image, and he again acquiesces. This act of hypocrisy brings him little good, and it constantly undermines his attempts to find a significant relationship with any other woman.

At the end of the novel, after a series of personal and political tragedies, Munson realizes that his fall from power was brought about because the political process is inherently corrupting and because his idealism was debased by egotism and pride. Now, a broken man, his will to power, along with his will to live, deserts him. In a demoralized and trance-like state of mind, he returns to the Dolly Pond Church of God. All the agonies of his life flash before his eyes, and in a spirit of repentance and hysteria, he joins the snake handlers. He is bitten in the neck and dies. Even though he did not receive the power or grace to take up serpents, his last words are testaments to his awareness that the life of the spirit is the only true reality (Cheney, *The Image*).

Caroline Gordon, still his teacher, friend, and critic, gave him some excellent technical advice on this novel, along with a few religiously partisan reflections about its central weakness:

> In this book you have got hold of one of the biggest themes of modern times—perhaps *the* biggest theme. Several novels I've read since I read yours fumble about with it, present it in part. You are the only one who's tackled it head-on. But damn it, you were too head-on. You were so impetuous that you wouldn't stop to consider the limitations of your medium. The reader's psychology is the instrument upon which you are giving your concert. You simply won't take it into enough account.
>
> Having got in this far I may as well be hanged for a sheep as a lamb. You have another handicap. You are ahead of your contemporaries in many ways. At present you are half in, half out of the Protestant *mystique*. You are not yet writing from the Christian mystique but you are dissatisfied with the Protestant mystique, as your book shows. If you were more at ease in your theology you'd have much less trouble with your technique (Gordon, "To Brainard Cheney").

Cheney felt that he had only partially succeeded in revealing the dilemmas of political life and that he had completely failed in his attempt to integrate the religious dimension into the novel. No matter how hard he worked on it, the beginning and end had a tacked-on, *deus ex machina* effect. Nevertheless, the religious affirmation seemed essential; it was the only answer that Cheney could see for Munson, a man whose ideals were unattainable in the temporal world.

Cheney never found a publisher for *The Image and the Cry*. Several editors were impressed by the novel's dramatic and realistic portrayal of the political world, yet most sensed Cheney's failure to integrate the novel's religious and political dilemmas.

Cheney's Contribution to All The King's Men

Even though he was unable to successfully bring off his own political novel, Cheney was able to give significant help to Robert Penn Warren in his writing of *All The King's Men*. The two men had continued their friendship over the years, visiting each other whenever their travels led them to the same vicinity, exchanging novels for critical reading, and corresponding from time to time about mutual friends, political events, and local gossip. Warren sent his first draft of *All The King's Men* to Cheney in October of 1945. He was aware of Cheney's vast experience in politics, and he knew that he could count on him to detect any false notes in his novel.

In fact, it could be argued that Warren's protagonist, Jack Burden, was partially modeled on the life of Cheney. Both were reporters for Southern newspapers who became attached to ambitious political leaders. Cheney worked as a reporter on the *Nashville Banner* from 1925 to 1942 and as a political aide and speechwriter for Senator Tom Stewart from 1943 to 1944 and later for the charismatic Governor of Tennessee Frank Clement from 1952-1958. Both Cheney and Jack Burden were from established Southern families and educated at Southern institutions. Both became disillusioned idealists, cynical about human nature and the prospects of enlightened political leadership. Of course, as is the case with most fiction, protagonists are often composites of many people that the author has known, integrated with parts of the author's own personality, thoughts, feelings and imaginative powers.

Cheney read the early draft and in November of that year wrote Warren a detailed, eight-page typewritten analysis of the novel, with comments and creative suggestions. Because Warren knew that Cheney had an authentic sense of the realities of the political world and a trained ear for political stump speeches, he incorporated nearly all of Cheney's ideas and language into his final version of *All the King's Men*. Fortunately, this exchange of letters has been preserved in the Cheney papers in the Special Collections Department of the Vanderbilt Library.

Robert Penn Warren, author of *All the King's Men* and long-time friend and confidant of Brainard Cheney. (*Courtesy Vanderbilt University Special Collections*)

After some beginning remarks in Cheney's November letter about the political effects of the schoolhouse disaster on Willie Stark's career, Cheney advised Warren to toughen up Sadie Burke's confrontation with Stark and to make Stark's confession to the people more dramatic:

Page 38: the you-sap initiation Sadie gives Willie—I feel that for an Irish girl and veteran of politics she manifests a poverty of political epithet: you might vary the term some, and build up to it by use of such synonyms as, "stalking horse" (of course stalking horses usually are not framed ones) "wooden-headed decoy," "sacrificial goat" (possibly, who thought he was the "lamb of God"—a little too wild perhaps). Of course his situation is so anomalous that the argot is a little limited for his case, but I offer those offhand.

Now for Willie's confession: Page 50 — As I said, it is now credible—by the hardest—but you still play too rough with Willie's vanity and that of his listeners—moreover I feel that you are again forgetting the significance of the modified schoolhouse episode and, perhaps, Willie's political instincts (those that he so profoundly manifests later at any rate). His matter of confession is too much like that of a soul-tortured priest, not a man of action's—which is (man of action) I take it, what he is, however, confused he may be about this himself at this juncture? (Cheney, "To Robert Penn Warren")

In the next part of the letter, Cheney does something unusual; he shifts his mode of critical discourse from analysis to narrative. Trying to explain to Warren what is wrong with Stark's speech, Cheney, as a writer himself, begins to create the actual speech as he thinks it should sound. This process results in a four page section of suggested narrative that Warren found so good and so in keeping with his conception of Stark that he used nearly all of it in his novel.

Here is a rough revision, which tries to suggest what I [Cheney] have in mind: (Beginning 3rd pg., p. 51)

He began again. "It is a funny story," he said. "Get ready to laugh and bust your sides for it's sure a funny story. A funny story if you can laugh at it!"

"It's about a hick—it's about a redneck, like yourselves, if you please. He grew up like any other mother's son on the dirt roads and gulley washes of a North State farm. And he knew what it was to get up before day and feed and slop and milk so he could set off by sunup to walk six miles to a one-room, slab-sided school house. He knew what it was to pay high taxes for that windy, shack of a schoolhouse and those gully-washed red-clay roads to walk over—and to break his wagon axles and stringhalt his mules on" (Cheney, "To Robert Penn Warren").

The Warren version as it appears in its final form in the novel is nearly a word-for-word incorporation.

Willie paused, and blinked around at the crowd. "No," he said, "I'm not going to read you any speech. You know what you need better'n I could tell you. But I'm going to tell you a story."

He begun again. "It's a funny story," he said. "Get ready to laugh. Get ready to bust your sides for it is sure a funny story. It's about a hick. It's about a red-neck, like you all, if you please. Yeah, like you. He grew up like any other mother's son on the dirt roads and gully washes of a north-state farm. He knew all about being a hick. He knew what it was to get up before day and get cow dung between his toes and feed and slop and milk before breakfast so he could set off by sunup to walk six miles to a one-room, slab-sided schoolhouse. He knew what it was to pay high taxes for that windy shack of a schoolhouse and those gully-washed red-clay roads to walk over—or to break his wagon axle or stringhalt his mules on." (Warren 97)

A further comparison of Cheney's 1945 letter with other sections of Warren's Chapter II shows that Cheney's ideas, idioms, and speech rhythms are followed with little modification. Often phrases, sentences, and portions of paragraphs are transcribed exactly. In the eight-page letter, Cheney continued to suggest what Stark would say at this political rally:

He knew what it is to be a hick, winter and summer. He figured if he wanted anything he had to do it for himself. So he sat up nights and studied law and, by the hardest, went to college some to get what they could give him there. So maybe he could be a lawyer and change things some. For himself and for others like him. I am not lying to you. Maybe, he didn't start out thinking about the other so much, but it come to him along the way that he could not do much for himself and his own without help from others—it had to be altogether, or none.

And it come to him with the powerful force of God's lightning on a tragic time in his own home county house years back, when the first brick school house—built out of rotten, politics-rotten brick—in his county seat collapsed and killed and mangled a dozen poor little scholars, and them mostly country ones. I won't get into that pitiful story—you've heard about it, I'm sure. But he had fought the corrupt politics of that schoolhouse-building and it got him started thinking on the cruel evil of the system that would let such a thing happen and he decided that any change that amounted to anything had to begin at the top, with those highest up.

When that schoolhouse tragedy transpired and helpless, innocent blood was spilled, people in his home county and everywhere remembered the hard, the failing fight he had made and held up his hand and said, "Here's an honest man who fought corruption without compromise—if we'd only listened to him!" And among them were some of the so-called political leaders of this State—some were said to be high minded and public spirited.

Then a time came, when another election for Governor was at hand, and some of these self-same public leaders came down to see the hick in Mason County. They were city big shots and rode in a high powered automobile, but they were the sheep's clothing of good country talk about honesty in government and a fair deal for the farmer. They said the state wanted a change, that it wanted a man whose honesty was proven and could be relied on to bring it about.

Yes sir, they told him they wanted him to be Governor and that they'd back him and he swallowed it. He looked into his heart and he knew that what they talked about he wanted more than anybody and he swallowed their sweet talk hook-line-and-sinker. He was just a human, country boy, who believed like we have always believed up here in the hills, that even the plainest, poorest fellow can be Governor if his fellow citizens find his character and his ideas right and pick him for the job.

So they came to pappy's house in that long automobile, wearing their striped pants and stiff-front shirts and said the State needed him and talked big about how much they could do to help him win. Boys, they said MacMurfee was a limber-back and a deadhead and that Harrison was the tool of the city machine, the city underworld, not the decent people. And he was hick enough to believe that there were some decent people in the city who wanted honest government, that there were some honest politicians, too, and that they might get out the decent and honest vote down there— to win an election.

He knew what they were saying about MacMurfee and Harrison was true—and God knows, he wanted a change to honest government. He looked in his heart and he said he be the man. Boys, they seen they had a hick and they taken him in—they taken him in, for they were, under their sheep's clothes, they were Joe Harrison's henchmen—straight from the city gang.

And the honesty and good government they wanted to practice was to split the country vote up here so that city-slick, Judas Joe Harrison could squeeze into the Governor's chair. They wanted a hick to lead the hicks away from Sam MacMurfee and elect Joe. That was what they wanted, that is all they want now—that is what they hope for, or did till I started talking to you here. And that is all you would accomplish if I stayed in this race and you voted for me.

I may be a hick, but by God I'm not a crook and nobody's going to make me one. They'll tell you that in Mason County. I am a hick, I'm of the hicks, and I'm for the hicks and it shall never be said of me that I misled them! Etcetera.

After this suggestion for the book, Cheney continued:

That's a very rough job, Red, and windy, but I believe it gets somewhere near where it should and that is one tenable ground for mitigation of "political stupidity" (a prime sin among men of action).

One thing more and I'm through: page 55, the word "crucify" won't do in that connection. The great unwashed reserve crucify for martyrdom. You can say drown him, or bury him under an avalanche of votes, or anything of the sort, but not crucify.

Oh yes, one little thing more. At bottom of page 56—I
believe it would go better if you would introduce that transition with some such phrase as you use on the next page,
like, "I didn't see or hear of Willie again after the campaign
..."

As you see I have spoken very freely and glibly—and now
I have the jitters about it—but I'm going to let this go ahead.
I know I can rely on you to pick out of this anything that
makes sense and suits your ends and throw the rest away
(Cheney, "To Robert Penn Warren").

Cheney's contribution seems more important when one realizes that this speech is one of the key scenes in the early part
of the novel. It represents the death of Stark's innocence and
the birth of his political career. From that moment, he is transformed from an idealistic dupe to a shrewd politician, and he
uses again and again the strategy that Cheney outlined—the
strategy of identification. It's as if Stark were saying: I'm one of
you, and the rich politicians think we are country hicks to be
used. Elect me, and we will show them how a hick can fight.

Warren acknowledged the help he received from Cheney in
two letters. In November of 1945 he wrote: "[I am returning]
Chapter II of my novel in its revised form in the hope that you
will find time to give it another look. This is, of course, the
chapter which needed most attention. If you have any thoughts,

scribble them in the margins or back. I have tried to meet your objections and incorporate your suggestion" (Warren, "To Brainard Cheney"). And again, seven months later, Warren wrote:

> I was pleased to learn that you have really gone to the mat with the new novel [*The Image and the Cry*]. I hope that it goes along. And you can count on one reader of your past work who looks forward with no common interest and expectation to the coming book. I almost worked up my courage to the point of sending my proofs to you for a final going-over of Willie, but I pride myself on having just enough decency to control my impulse and to allow you to attend to your own affairs without having to do more of my work for me. So the thing is now sealed up, for better or worse. And I repeat my thanks for your invaluable assistance. (Warren, "To Brainard Cheney")

Over the years, Warren read all of Cheney's novels in their early drafts, and he aided him substantially with critical comments, suggestions, and ideas. It must have given Cheney a great sense of satisfaction to be able to help Warren in his writing of *All the King's Men*, one of Warren's best works and one of the finest political novels of our time.

CHAPTER VII
Religion, Politics, and Polemics

During the years after his Washington experience when he
was wrestling with *The Image and the Cry* and the problems of
political dealism, Cheney began to see that political life was not
only corrupting but also shortsighted and transitory. Was it not
foolish for one to put his faith in imperfect men, motivated by
selfish political aims? And was not the Utopian dream of prosperity for all misguided and ridiculous when one faced the final
fact of existence—personal death?

Cheney's new awareness of the limitations of political and
social action and his increasing need for permanent and com-
prehensive answers led him inevitably to religion—the storehouse of man's best answers to the ultimate questions of life.

He read accounts of all the major world religions—Hinduism, Judaism, Islam, and Buddhism. The Eastern ways of thought, however, remained strange and unsatisfying to him. He discovered that he could not divorce himself from his cultural and intellectual heritage. Christianity had been the dominant myth of his civilization and Catholicism, he thought, was its first and truest expression (Cheney, Interview 11 April).

Other than being the purest and most fundamental form of Christianity, Catholicism had many other elements in it that appealed to Cheney. The artist in him responded to the vast and intricate symbolism of the Church, and he began to see the rituals as dramatic acts—especially the mass, which was a spiritual reenactment of Christ's death and resurrection. He also began to think that life at its most fundamental level was not physical and material, but spiritual and supernatural. "But what I am now thoroughly convinced of is man's super nature—in fact, all life, perhaps, is possessed of an element of super nature, which is—to speak of something figuratively, sense-bound that I am—the hand of God holding it in organization. But once you become aware of the supernatural, it seems incredible that you should ever have been so unconscious of its presence—it is so surely and so obviously there, although, prisoned as you are by your senses, it is difficult to describe that fifth dimension which exists neither in time nor space—but gives all form, all existence, all being" (Cheney, "To Robert Penn Warren").

The idea of God began to fulfill his deepest need for a sense of order, meaning, and purpose in the universe and in his personal life.

> Metaphysically, when I say God, I am talking about (I think) that mysterious quality of the universe—The Whole, apprehensible and conceivable to man—that is called meaning.
>
> This God-symbol has a consequent significance for man, that of purpose, cosmic purpose, in which his part is to discover the meaning of the universe and his share in it. This is the moral, or what I call the dramatic view of the universe, without which, I believe history demonstrates, man falls into confusion and decay. (Cheney, "To Tommy Stritch")

He began to see that the ultimate quest of life was a union of the individual's life with God, and that the life of Christ was "the way."

> It is [Eric] Neumann's impressive conclusion that the ego first found maturity and continues to find maturity in controversion (to use his word) in the ego's voluntary reunion with the total psyche. To be sure Jesus Christ dramatized controversion in the history of the Western World—Christ, memorialized and ritually preserved to Christians in

the sacrament of the Eucharist. So, the soul, under Christ's direction, sought maturity, or Christianity, in a deliberate submersion of the ego in the total psyche, through His aid and example.

It seems to me that controversion, under Christ's example and by His grace, takes the most complete view of man's predicament on this earth and directs him toward his greatest potentiality.

And so, this dimension of human life called direction, under Christianity, proposes to lead a man from ego obsession to the love of his fellow man for the love of God and by way of grace to self-transcendence and eventual union with God—that is, the Beatific Vision. And, it should be added, by this Way, transcendence of death, too—transcendence of time and space, in eternity. (Cheney, "To Dick Beatty")

The Roman Catholic Church with its long history and enriched symbols and myths brought solace to the minds of many of the post-war generation. To the intellectuals of the modern wasteland, disillusioned and alienated from their own nuclear age, the church gave a sense of unity and continuity with the past and an older vision of life from which to draw strength.

Following the lead of T. S. Eliot and other intellectuals, Allen and Caroline Tate joined the Catholic Church. In a March 1950 edition of the Partisan Review, the editors state, "one of the most significant tendencies of our time, especially in this

decade, has been the new turn toward religion among intellectuals and the growing disfavor with which secular attitudes and
perspectives are now regarded in not a few circles that lay claim
to the leadership of culture." ("Religion and the Intellectuals").

The Tates conversion made a deep impression on Cheney,
and in the next few years, their gentle persuasion took its effect.
Caroline Gordon was sometimes more than gentle in her advo-
cacy, and on a few occasions, her newfound religious feelings
eclipsed her otherwise excellent critical advice to Cheney. "You
placed your hero [Bob Munson] up against a half truth (Holy
Rollerism is a half truth.) If you had placed him in relation to
the real truth, in relation to the one holy Church, Christ's Mys-
tical Body on earth, your plot would have worked better. But
you couldn't do that because you yourself aren't sure in your
faith" (Gordon, "To Brainard Cheney). Tate, on the other hand,
was more subtle in his attempts to influence Cheney toward the
church. "As you will remember, I told you that I thought you
had reached the stage at which no persuasion or argument
should be dealt out to you: the Decision must be made at your
advanced position all alone. BUT if you are thinking of taking
the step very soon, I merely suggest that the Retreat would be a
good place for it. Father Hugh Duffy, the Prior of the monas-

tery, could officiate and we could sponsor you if you wanted us" (Tate, "To Brainard Cheney). It was not, however, until 1953 that Cheney made up his mind, received instruction from Monsignor Albert Siener, rector of the Cathedral of Incarnation in Nashville, and entered the Catholic Church.

Christian Political Realism

In 1952, a few months before his religious conversion, Cheney accepted a position as speechwriter and director of public relations for Tennessee's Governor Frank Clement. This office put Cheney back into the political arena after a seven-year retreat.

Cheney worked well with Clement because their religious and political views were largely compatible. Clement was a dynamic and progressive governor for Tennessee. He blended "personal religious fervor with astute politics—plus some constructive reforms in mental-hospital facilities, education (free textbooks), and standardized methods of state purchasing" (Dykeman 49). Dykeman characterized him in an article for *Harper's Magazine* as:

Six feet tall, with dark curly hair, intense eyes and a frequent handsome smile. Clement might be described as a political evangelist. He interprets the *Bible* literally, the Constitution literally, and never forgets that more Tennesseans
attend Wally Fowler's All-Night Sings (of hillbilly ballads
and hymns) than listen to all the symphonic music in the
state. His compelling power as a public speaker, which has
aroused expressions of appreciation and commendation
from party leaders all over the nation, stems from a kind of
modern-dress revival of the William Jennings Bryan type of
oratory. And it seems possible that, just as Bryan was
known as "silver-tongued," so this stout advocate of TVA
may become famous as "electrifying." (49)

Clement's career was long and impressive. He was elected
governor for three terms, a total of ten years in that office.
Cheney was with Clement from 1952 to 1958 and helped him
win in the 1954 primary "the largest majority vote ever given a
gubernatorial candidate in Tennessee" (Dykeman 49). By 1956,
he had become a national figure, campaigning through the
country for his fellow Democrats, singing the praises of TVA
and blasting away at the Eisenhower administration.

Alan Griggs, a political researcher at Western Kentucky
University, says of Cheney's role as a speechwriter in the Clement's administration, "Cheney, known for his strength as a researcher, utilized his many contacts across Tennessee to pro-

vide anecdotes for Clement's speeches. He visited towns soon to host Clement and talked with the local folks, brought that information back to the state capitol, and put it into speeches. While his writing seemed too erudite for Clement, he played a major role in developing the governor's public stands on issues, especially his strong defense of the Tennessee Valley Authority.

Tennessee Governor Frank Clement (second from left) with Adlai Stevenson at the 1956 Democratic convention.

Cheney was one of several speechwriters who helped craft Governor Clement's dramatic keynote address at the Democratic National Convention of 1956 that resulted in his name being put forward as a possible running mate with Adlai Stevenson. Other nominees to the Vice President position were Estes Kefauver, Albert Gore, Sr., Hubert Humphrey, and the young Senator from Massachusetts, John F. Kennedy. After a hotly debated balloting process, the delegates chose Estes Kefauver, the U.S. Senator from Tennessee, to be Stevenson's running mate. The Stevenson ticket, however, was roundly beaten by the popular Republican incumbents, Dwight Eisenhower and Richard Nixon.

It was rumored that Governor Clement would run for president in 1960, but his prospects for future national politics, were dimmed by questions of his religious sincerity and rumors of heavy drinking during his last term of office as governor (1962-66). He died in an automobile accident in 1969 ("Obituary of Frank G. Clement").

In addition to being actively engaged in the politics of Tennessee, Cheney began during these years to publish his own political thoughts in a series of religious and political essays. The emptiness that resulted from the loss of his early political idealism had been filled, since his conversion, by his new religious perspective. In a series of articles "The Leader Follows—Where?" (1948), "Conservatives Course by Celestial Navigation" (1954), "A new Crown of Thorns for the Democratic Party" (1956), and "Christianity and the Tragic Vision" (1961), he outlined his doctrine of Christian Political Realism. In these essays, he expressed the view that the political liberals—with their radical belief in the ultimate goodness of man and the perfectibility of the human predicament, with their planned societies, gospels of progress through science, and their belief in Utopianism—heaven on *this* earth—were unrealistic, false, and misguiding. Man's life on earth is physically tragic, for his unavoidable destiny is death. All life dies, but only man, among the species, "knows" his ultimate faith.

Cheney wrote further in these articles that materialism, the obsession of the twentieth century, is a false God that distracts man from his ultimate concern. The best that one can hope for in the political world is Christian Realism. While advocating tolerance toward all, a Christian Realist understands that man is often motivated by greed rather than concern for his fellows. A Christian Realist does not believe in "sentimental democracy," the idea that governments truly serve the governed. He knows that the democratic ideal is an illusion and that political reality consists of squabbling lobbyists and special interest groups who are only concerned with their own welfare. The Christian realist would direct men away from their obsessive interest in the affairs of this world to a concern for their souls. He would caution the world leaders against following the morality and opinion pollsters who record the selfish interest of humanity, rather than the common good. He would admonish them to follow the divine fundamental laws of life, the Christian ideals of love, charity, justice, and brotherhood, and, above all, to beware of the sin of pride—man's belief that through his own powers he can save himself (Cheney, "Christianity and the Tragic Vision").

Although anti-liberal in most of his views after 1945, Cheney's conservatism was qualified in two important ways. Whereas most conservatives have such an abiding distrust of the federal government that they seek to limit its activity on every possible front, Cheney believed that in certain areas, it not only had a legitimate right to operate but that it was sometimes the only agency that could do the job. For example, he did not support Donald Davidson's view that the federal government should stay out of producing, selling, and regulating electric power and other sources of public energy within a state (Davidson, "To Brainard Cheney"). In fact, Cheney helped Clement draw up a strong position in support of TVA. In numerous speeches, they warned the voters that the power production of the nation was so vital to the national interest that it must not fall into the hands of large, private, often monopolistic, corporations.

> No administration must be permitted to turn back the clock—or to return this country to a condition of high electric rates and power scarcity—of making the power industry private chattel of the private power monopoly without the restraints of public power competition . . . . I am one who believes that the TVA will go down in history as the greatest American political invention for regional administrative government—and the salvation of the power industry (Clement, Address).

The second qualification of Cheney's conservatism was that he did not share with his Agrarian friends the belief that America could return to an antebellum style of life, nor did he agree with their tacit approval of a separate and unequal status for the African-American citizens. Cheney had seen enough poverty in rural Georgia to make him unwilling to accept any idyllic dreams of a new Agrarian culture for the South, and his personal relationship with his friend, Robin Bess, an African American man, helped him to understand the unfairness and inequity of Southern feudalism.

In a review of *The Lasting South*, a collection of essays by Southern Conservatives, Cheney sharply pointed out the limitations of an Agrarian position:

> The South was an anachronism in Western society by the middle of the nineteenth century.
>
> There was sentimentality in the old South's view of the nature of its way of life and in its blindness to the shortcomings of this way. This same exaggeration of values and blindness, I believe, is generally implicit in *I'll Take My Stand* and in *The Lasting South*. . .I may add that it was and astonishingly continues to be a part of this blindness in the recent symposium [*The Lasting South*] that these Southerners underrate the power and fail to see the reach of industrialism.
>
> An idea that will increase a man's productivity, in his post-Eden predicament, a hundredfold, cannot humanly be turned back. I think our political experience has proven that we've got to treat with this idea. We can most realistically do that by trying to understand it, then to direct it and qualify its significance.
>
> We have got to go back further into our origins, our source of motivation, than to the tradition of the gentleman, Southern or otherwise. We have got to conjure with greater

Power. We have got to go back to our Christian heritage. (Cheney, "What Endures in the South")

These important qualifications of Cheney's conservatism leave us with a picture of a complex man; a seasoned politician who, after the destruction of his early political idealism, found renewed hope in a religious vision of life. Clearly, Cheney is a man whose diverse political views escape convenient labeling. While he is optimistic about the future and man's ultimate reward, he is pessimistic about human nature, America's insatiable appetite for consumer goods, and the nation's unguided industrial growth. While he is liberal in his attitudes toward African Americans, civil rights issues, and responsible federal government, he is conservative in his distrust of science, materialistic goals, and public mores established not by religious authority but by the mass media and public opinion polls. This array of complex views is unified by Cheney's unswerving belief in the absolute verities of the Christian faith and by his steadfast conviction that man should pay more attention to the fate of his soul than the fortunes of the state.

Religion and Art

In 1950, Cheney decided to try his hand at playwriting. He extracted the snake-handling episode out of his political novel, *The Image and the Cry,* and wrote an independent drama from the material. He changed most of the events and principal characters, but kept the original setting and the religious theme. He called his new play, *Strangers in This World.*

The stage directions for the opening scene gave the setting:

TIME: Afternoon of summer of 1943.

PLACE: Interior of Dolly Pond Church, in Grasshopper Valley, Tennessee County, Tennessee. It is a tiny, unpainted, unsealed room with 12 rows of benches on either side of a middle aisle. At one end is outside entrance, at other a low dais, at front of which is a plank pulpit or lectern. On the dais, in split-bottomed chairs, sit the saints-choir-chorus: men in overalls and women in calico dresses. The benches are well filled. A coffin, on sawhorses and covered with mountain flowers, lies before the pulpit.

THE OCCASION: The funeral of Lonnie Pippin who has been bitten by a snake at a snake-handling rite and has died. (Cheney, *Strangers in This World*)

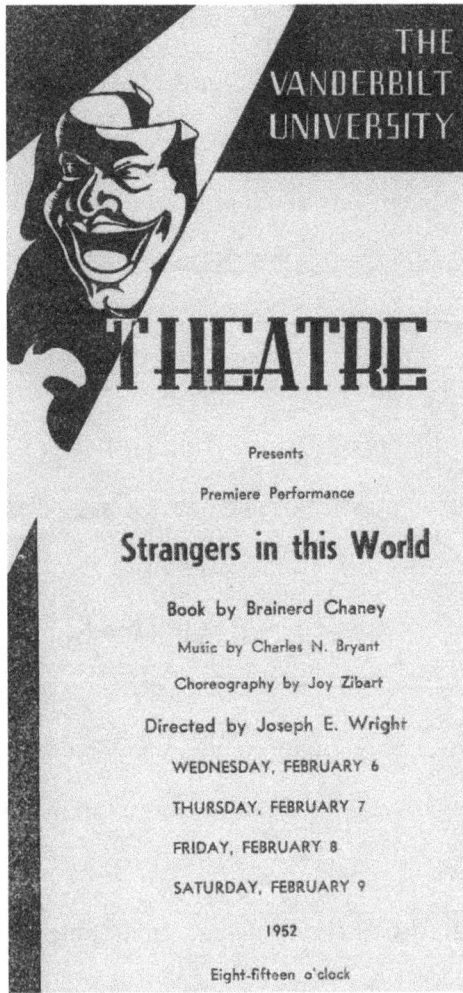

THE
VANDERBILT
UNIVERSITY

THEATRE

Presents

Premiere Performance

Strangers in this World

Book by Brainerd Chaney

Music by Charles N. Bryant

Choreography by Joy Zibart

Directed by Joseph E. Wright

WEDNESDAY, FEBRUARY 6

THURSDAY, FEBRUARY 7

FRIDAY, FEBRUARY 8

SATURDAY, FEBRUARY 9

1952

Eight-fifteen o'clock

Cheney's play, *Strangers in this World,* was presented at Vanderbilt in 1952 to good reviews. The choreographer was family friend, Joy Zibart. (*Courtesy Vanderbilt University Special Collections*)

The church is visited by the county sheriff and Jack Day, a newspaper reporter for the *Chattanooga News*. Word has spread about the death of one of the snake handlers, and the outside world is curious about this strange religious cult. The sheriff, who thinks that snake-handling should be outlawed in the state, has been sent out to investigate the case, and Jack Day, cynical, unreligious, and modern, is there to cover the story for the *Chattanooga News*.

During the course of the play, Jack Day becomes attracted to Virgie Noland, a young hill woman of great beauty. She is lured by Jack's sophistication and promises of an exciting life in the city. Yet she doubts his sincerity and is also drawn to Lige Born, the elderly founder and spiritual leader of the Dolly Pond Church of God. Lige promises her a family, respect, and a life of the Spirit.

Lige had started the cult of snake handling thirty years before. One evening while he was walking through the woods, he had heard the terrifying sound of a nearby rattlesnake. The biblical passage—"And these signs shall follow them that believe: in my name shall they cast out devils, they shall speak with new tongues, they shall take up serpents"—flashed through his mind. He dropped down on his hands and knees, "a-scared and a-quakin," called out to God, and received the anointment of the "Power." He took up the deadly rattler and put it to his face and then to his forehead. He was unharmed by the snake; his faith in God and the power of the spirit had been vindicated.

The plot of *Strangers in This World* becomes complicated by the passing of a state law against the snake handling practice, by Jack's successful seduction of Virgie, and by a doctrinaire split in the church over the way to handle the snakes—wildly and chaotically, which sometimes results in a death, or with a sense of order, as Lige recommends. Virgie, who is the central character in the play, marries the elderly spiritual leader but finds neither peace nor happiness. She is tormented by not knowing whether the child she bears is Lige's or Jack's, and she is afraid that her sin with Jack has prevented her from receiving the power to take up serpents.

The play reaches its climax during a snake-handling session when one of the radical members of the church thrusts a snake upon the unprepared Virgie. In a state of excitement and fear, Lige grabs the snake from her before he has received the Power. The snake strikes him mortally, and he falls to the floor.

Virgie runs hysterically from the church, followed by Jack, who promises to marry her if she will give up her fanatic beliefs. She refuses him and climbs through the woods to the mountain top where Lige first took up snakes. She too receives the anointment from God and in an act of faith and belief takes up a serpent. By this act, she becomes the new spiritual leader of the Dolly Pond Church of God (Cheney, *Strangers in This World*).

Strangers in This World was produced by the Vanderbilt University Theater in February 1952 as a folk drama with music and dance. Charles Bryan of the department of music at Peabody College provided the music, and Joy Zibart created the dance. The play was considered one of the most successful productions of the Vanderbilt University Theater (Cox, *Strangers in This World*). The presence of live snakes electrified the audience, and Virgie's final hilltop dance made a sensational ending. Four years later, the play was presented to a capacity audience (including Tennessee's Governor Clement and his staff) in Louisville, Kentucky, by the University of Louisville Playhouse. That production, directed by John Caldwell, received not only local acclaim but several favorable reviews by the national press. From time to time, Broadway producers have shown interest in *Strangers in This World*, but as of today, it has not had a New York showing.

Strangers in This World, like Cheney's political novel, suffered from his struggle to come to terms with his religion. The play was first produced three years before his conversion. After his conversion in 1953, he began to worry about its pagan implications. Some of his Catholic spiritual and intellectual advisors felt that the play had heretical elements in it and that the Christian import was not clear (Cheney, "To Father Gilbert V. Hartke"). Cheney rewrote the play several times, trying to make its meaning more consistent with his Christian beliefs. He reduced Virgie's central role in the drama to a secondary position. In the revised play, she is merely a wayward girl who repents and is forgiven of her sins. The new protagonist is Lige, the founder of the church who becomes a Christ-like figure, for he dies to save Virgie from the snake, and he forgives both Jack and Virgie of their sexual transgression. Henry Samples, a New York producer who was once interested in the play, objected to Cheney's rewritten version. He especially disliked the last scene which he felt was straining for a Christian effect (Samples, "To Brainard Cheney").

Cheney admitted that his religious zeal probably hurt the play. His dilemma with *Strangers* was that although the play was a powerful existential statement of the existence of the spiritual world, theologically, it was inconsistent with his Catholic ideology. He could not dramatically link snake-handling with the mission of Christ. On a spiritual and intuitive level, they were connected, but theologically they were incompatible. Cheney wrote a third version that brought the play back to its original form, back to its simple and powerful affirmation of the spiritual world.

The relationship between art and religion is a thorny aesthetic problem, and Cheney wrestled with it for many years in his writing of *The Image and the Cry* and *Strangers in This World*. In *Art and Human Values*, Melvin Rader sheds some light on the problem. "If religious meanings are to be genuinely aesthetic, they must function as an integral part of the work. If, on the contrary, religious symbolism pulls us away from the aesthetic surface and substitutes external reference for intrinsic beauty and signification, it is a corrupting influence in art" (Rader and Jessup 204). Flannery O'Connor, on one of her many visits to Idler's Retreat, advised Cheney not to let his religion call attention to itself.

John Crowe Ransom develops a helpful metaphor in an article called "Poets without Laurels." He suggests that the combinations of the moral and aesthetic element can be thought of as

assemblages ["lumps of morality and image lying side by side"],
mixtures, or compounds. Ransom prefers works of art that integrate art and morality into a compound state. "The effect
which we actually receive from the poetry is not that of an ag-
gregate or series or mechanical mixture of distinct properties
but only the single effect of a compound. In that event the
properties will exist separate only in our minds, by a later act of
qualitative analysis, and they will not really be in the poetry in
their own identities" (Ransom 728).

In this difficult period in his life, from the end of his Washington years in 1945 to his resignation from Frank Clement's
staff in 1958, Cheney underwent great changes in his political
and religious thinking. In his conception of Christian Realism,
he was able to achieve a successful synthesis of his political and
religious thought. But his attempt to integrate religion and art
was not as successful. His political novel, *The Image and the
Cry*, was a failure, and his religious play *Strangers in This
World*, although a local success, never fulfilled its promise.
Cheney's works of literature during this period were, in Ransom's metaphor, aesthetic mixtures. They were landmarks in
his spiritual odyssey, rather than unified and finished works of
art. Cheney's later novels, although containing some religious

dimensions, are not burdened with theological doctrine. In them, he is more successful in achieving a fusion of the moral and dramatic elements into aesthetic "compounds."

CHAPTER VIII

This is Adam

A Novel of Grace and Duty in
the Segregated South

Cheney's retirement from politics in 1958 marked the beginning of his most productive period of literary accomplishments. In the following eleven years, from 1958 to 1969, he published essays on Teilhard de Chardin and Arnold Toynbee; literary articles on the achievements of Flannery O'Connor, Caroline Gordon, and Peter Taylor; and book reviews for the *Sewanee Review* and the *Nashville Banner*.

Cheney also wrote and helped produce a play, *I Choose to Die*, in this period. It was a drama based on the life of the Confederate hero, Sam Davis, with a dance interlude directed by Joy Zibart. The play was performed by the Vanderbilt University Theater in Nashville in November of 1960. In addition to this play, literary essays, articles, and reviews, Cheney completed the most ambitious literary project of his career—a trilogy of novels.

In the earlier novels, *Lightwood* and *River Rogue*, Cheney had written about the distant past of Georgia; in his new trilogy, *This is Adam*, *Quest of the Pelican*, and *Devil's Elbow*, he turned, like other American writers—Wolfe, Hemingway, Fitzgerald, and Anderson—to his own personal history for material. In *The Novel Today*, critic David Lodge writes that while many authors use materials from their past, their personal experience is "explored and transmuted until it acquires an authenticity and persuasiveness independent of its actual origins" (Lodge 108).

From the experiences of his life, Cheney forged a fictional world that captured people and events from his boyhood days in Georgia to his political career in Tennessee, a world that, through its created order and design, expressed his personal insights into the nature of man and the significance of human events.

The two protagonists of the novel, Adam Atwell, an African American man, and Lucy Hightower, the owner of a large tract of land, were beseeched by unscrupulous land speculators.

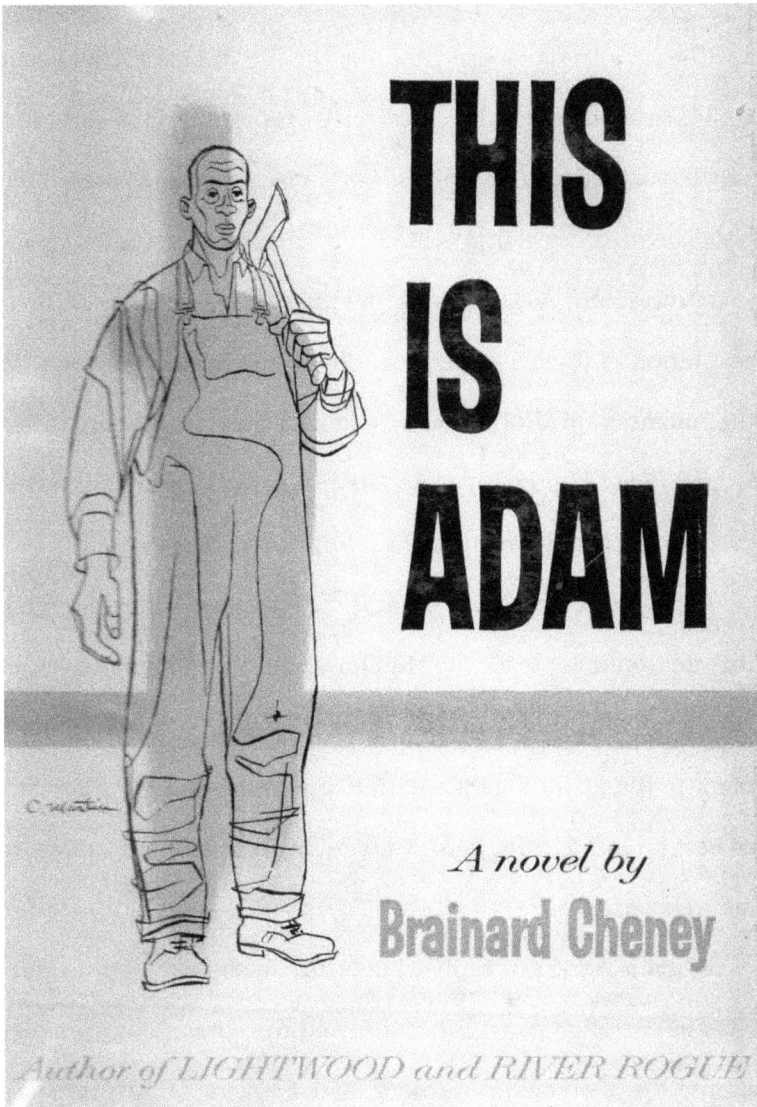

Original cover for Brainard Cheney's third novel, published in 1958. It tells a fictionalized version of the story of his mother and the family's overseer, Adam Atwell. They "transacted a world across a flight of steps that separated them in manifest social accommodation and joined them in an inscrutable fate."

This is Adam

Cheney's trilogy loosely follows the life of Marse Hightower from boyhood to middle age. *This is Adam*, the first and most successful of the three novels, takes place during Marse's boyhood in 1910; its central characters are Marse's mother, Lucy Hightower, and Adam Atwell, the mixed-race overseer of their plantation in Riverton, Georgia. Cheney dedicated the book "to the memory of Robin Bess, whose character inspired this work." (See Chapter I, "Early Life in Rural Georgia," for a discussion of Cheney's relationship with Robin Bess.)

Adam promised Marse's father, Marcellus, before he died, that he would not leave the Hightower family and that he would continue in his position as overseer, helping Mrs. Hightower manage the 1,800-acre plantation and protecting her interests, as best he could, from those who might try to take advantage of her inexperience.

When a Northern timber buyer becomes interested in purchasing the Hightower Plantation and the surrounding smaller farms, the merchants, farmers, and bankers of Riverton are jubilant over the prospects of seeing some "hard cash" come into the impoverished area. Mrs. Hightower is also excited because the sale of her estate will give her enough money to return to her childhood home in Charleston, South Carolina. As a girl, she had been raised in cultured Charleston, and she longs to go back to it, to be with her old friends, and to raise her son, Marse, in its civilizing atmosphere.

She has, however, two responsibilities that hinder her from an immediate sale of her lands. Before his death, Marcellus told her that a part of the land contained clay deposits that might someday be very valuable. To keep this prospect open for her son, a duty that she keenly feels, Mrs. Hightower insists on reserving the mineral rights on that portion of the land. She is further obligated to refrain from selling the cotton land that Adam farms. Ten years before, her husband had promised Adam that if he would come to Riverton and help with the plantation, he could farm the rich Wyche field as long as he wanted.

As in most Southern novels, the land in *This is Adam* is a powerful symbol. The Hightower Plantation stands as a physical manifestation of the moral responsibilities between the characters. When they want to sell the land, get rid of it, leave it, steal it, forsake it, they are, in essence, trying to break the bonds of their responsibilities to each other. But as Cheney shows, these responsibilities are not easily cast off; they are powerful and tenacious, haunting consciousness and transcending death.

These two stipulations of Mrs. Hightower on the land sale cool the interest of the Northern buyer and set off a chain of events that nearly result in Adam's death. The poor white farmers neighboring the Hightower Plantation try to force Adam to lie about the boundary lines of the Plantation and the location of the clay deposits. If he would agree to tell Mrs. Hightower that the clay deposits were located in an area of her land that the timber buyers were planning to lease rather than purchase, the land deal would go through, the neighbors would obtain a good price on their land, and Mrs. Hightower would sell not only her timber land but, unknowingly, her clay deposits as well. Adam, however, refuses to join this conspiracy and is consequently subjected to a series of increasingly hostile intimidations by members of the white community interested in promoting the land sale.

In Adam's resistance to the pressures that are brought against him, Cheney shows us a man of heroic stature. Adam is not only uncommonly shrewd and courageous but he possesses a personal integrity that cannot be compromised. It arises from his being true to his values, his sense of himself, and it is reflected in his ability to remain steadfast in his obligations to others. When Marcellus, Marse's father, makes his last request, Adam accepts the heavy responsibility without qualification.

> He managed to raise his head off the pillow. "But Adam, I hope I can depend on you with the farming and timbering on the homeplace. I am counting on you to advise her the best you know how and look after the place, regardless of who comes on it. I know it won't be easy, because of your color and your station. There will be a lot of barbed wire and picked padlocks in this—it will put you to the test many times. . . .There are others, it should be said, more properly placed to take this responsibility, but I confess to you that I don't have confidence in them. I've tested you, Adam: you take responsibility—and you know as much about the homeplace as anybody. . . .It's my last request." (Cheney, *This Is Adam* 21)

This scene is a "flashback" in time—a narrative technique that Cheney used extensively and skillfully. The present action of the novel takes place during three months in the summer of 1910. Through the memories of Adam and Mrs. Hightower, the reader learns of important events twenty and thirty years earlier—events from Adam's early life, his troubles with the law, Marcellus's defense of him, their plans to start a clay works industry, and Lucy Hightower's courtship and early marriage to

Marcellus, and her difficulty in adapting to the semi-barbarous south Georgia.

Adam's integrity and loyalty are severely tested through the course of the novel. As a Southern African American, his responsibility to the widow places him in a dangerous position. While trying to protect her interests, he must not alienate the white community; for in the South, in that period of time, an African American person could not expect to offend whites and either prosper economically or live in freedom from personal injury.

In one of the most poignant scenes in the novel, Cheney dramatizes Adam's attempt to walk this line between loyalty and diplomacy. The town banker, lawyer, and several farmers (one of whom holds a mortgage on the land Adam is buying) summon Adam to a meeting in a brightly lit backroom in a lawyer's office. The reader, who has grown to understand and respect Adam, suffers with him as he wavers between his fear of the hostile white men and his determination to remain loyal to Mrs. Hightower.

> Uncertain whether he should knock, loath to enter at all, he knocked twice and waited for the second sharp call to *Come in!* Before he opened the door. The same voice called

again, "In here!" And he found his way across the dark, empty front room and through an open door into a back room.

His eyes widened and his hat slipped out of his hand. His misgivings had not prepared him for what confronted him. The room blazed with blinding light from an electric lamp suspended from the ceiling at the center of it, and beyond the ball of brightness. . .were seated a row of white men that ran all the way around the room. . . .

"Adam, I guess you know why we sent for you?". . . "My clients here believe that Mrs. Hightower may have got her erroneous misconception from you". . . .

. . .the door in the side wall opened and Hinshaw Slappy entered the room. Looking in Adam's direction but avoiding his eye, he called "Hey there, Adam, I told them I thought you just got mixed up as betwixt which wuz which line!"

Swaying, Adam shifted his stance to steady himself. He saw on their faces that they all knew that Slappy was lying. And, wincing, he saw more: he saw that, though ashamed of it, they meant for *him* to pretend to believe Slappy, too!

Somebody said, "We all got to be together on this!"

Duke [the lawyer] leaned toward Adam, holding out his hand. "This understanding is going to be better for everybody," he said, and his smile seemed almost genuine.

Adam looked at the proffered hand, feeling the wall of pressure bearing down on him.

"I-I ho-hope so!" he stammered, wondering what he meant.

There was a laugh and someone said, "Shore as shootin'!" And the white men began to shove back their chairs and get up.

But Adam did not take Duke's hand. Instead he abruptly lowered his own hands to his sides and stood there trembling, his ginger-colored face, gray and pinched with fear, his eye-whites shoaling up. Bracing against the door, he said, in an intense smooth monotone: "Why don't y'all git the county surveyor to prove that line, white fo'ks?" (45-51)

Later in the novel, when it becomes clear to these men that Adam's loyalty to the Hightowers cannot be broken, they pay Kiger Steel, an African American and acquaintance of Adam's, to kill him, throw his body in the river, and claim that he drowned in a boating accident.

Despite Adam's heroic qualities of courage, shrewdness, and integrity, he, like Micajah Corn and Ratliff Sutton, is an insufficient hero. The dramatic situation that Cheney constructs in *This is Adam* calls for a hero. Mrs. Hightower, recently widowed, with a son to raise and an estate to protect, is like a modern-day Penelope, needing an Odysseus to return home, slay the avaricious suitors, and assume his position as husband and father. Being African American, uneducated, and poor, Adam is unable to fulfill this role; he is socially unfit, according to the social code of those times, to be Lucy Hightower's husband.

Although Mrs. Hightower never consciously considers Adam as a possible mate, Cheney delicately hints from time to time of an attraction between them. Each Saturday morning, Adam reports to Mrs. Hightower on the affairs of the Plantation: he, typically, at her porch, in her back yard, at the base of the steps to her house, looking up at her not deferentially but with a calm reserve. She, symbolically, at the top of the stairs, refined, Victorian, bewildered by the ordeal of running a plantation, and both hopeful yet skeptical of selling out and returning to Charleston.

Cheney uses these scenes on the porch steps of the Hightower home not just to symbolize the relationship between Adam and Mrs. Hightower but also to give structural unity to the novel. The plot of *This Is Adam* develops like two interweaving pieces of thread; one strand follows the experiences of Mrs. Hightower, the other follows Adam. Cheney unifies his story by bringing these lines together eight times, as Adam and Mrs. Hightower, at the porch steps of her house, exchange the most recent developments in their separate problems and are reminded of their responsibilities to each other.

This cover is from the 2012 reissue of *This Is Adam*. Photograph taken in Dodge County, Georgia in the early 1900s. The three characters parallel the three main actors in the novel. The woman on the porch is Nancy Hendley Hargrove, an ancestor of the publisher. *(Courtesy Jacque Hargrove Hardy)*

The narrator says of them that they transacted "a world across a flight of steps that separated them in manifest social accommodation and joined them in an inscrutable fate." After one of these ritual Saturday meetings, Mrs. Hightower's train of thought about Adam is broken by the small penetrating sound of a hummingbird as she sat on the porch alone:

> Her glance found the bird. Within the dim cloister, he hovered, a small feathered missile of changeable green and gray and scarlet, poised between two dark blurs of wings before an open red trumpet flower. Unmindful of her gaze, driven by his whirring power, he gracefully thrust with his long, slender, black beak down into the blossom. Then out again he darted, moving backward with the same swift grace, to poise in air. And, cocking his small head toward her, his tiny black beads of sight met the tender eyes in the white, still face, in an instant of mysterious recognition. (86)

Even though the sexual symbolism of the bird's actions is obvious, Mrs. Hightower's attraction to Adam is literally unthinkable for her. For a Southern woman of high breeding, marriage across racial and social barriers is anathema. Mrs. Hightower's mind quickly jerks itself away from Adam to Edward Louthan, a cultured white man from Charleston to whom she was once engaged and who has recently asked her to marry. Cheney has Mrs. Hightower make the change of context so quickly and smoothly that the association of the bird to Adam never fully enters her consciousness:

> Abruptly, the humming of the wings changed and he was gone.
>
> Lucy smiled and began to rock the big chair back and forth. *Wade Hampton marching by*! She repeated to herself absently, her previous anxiety now out of her mind. She might not have remembered the incident [a parade] but for Edward's poem about it later. (86)

Lucy Hightower is, however, fully conscious of her reliance and dependence on Adam. Without Adam as a protector and guardian, she knows she would be easy prey for the white townsmen who want to steal her land. When she thought of Adam,

> . . . she felt defended against all of the deceit and trickery who appeared to have joined together against her, merely because she had property and was a woman too inexperienced to protect it. . .Yes, thank God, there was one *man* in the lot! (105).

Besides protector and guardian, Adam is needed as a substitute father to the eleven-year-old Marse Hightower. Worried about her son's development, Mrs. Hightower frequently turns to Adam for help. He takes the boy hunting and fishing and gives him paternal advice and guidance. On one occasion, when Mrs. Hightower is out of town for two weeks, Adam allows Marse to stay with him on his farm. When Mrs. Hightower returns, Adam gently reassures her that the boy is growing into a responsible youth:

> "Yessum. Me and Marse got pretty well acquainted while you wuz gone." Adam nodded his head measuredly. "He growin' up and he growin' up all right. . . ."
>
> "He probably not goin' to be as big a man as his pa," Adam continued, conscious of the importance of his responsibilities. "But he goin' to be like 'im. Goin' to be like 'im where hit counts. . . . And whut he tell you, hits like that—you kin depend on it."
>
> Mrs. Hightower swallowed, her lips loosening, her face gathering in warmth. "I hope you know that nothing could please me more than to hear you say this, Adam!" (204-205)

Adam is, therefore, allowed to be Mrs. Hightower's protector and guardian and foster-father to her son, but because of his race and social position, he is inadequately qualified to be her husband.

In addition to his racial and social deficiencies, which are due to no fault of his own, Adam is less than an adequate hero because of a personal flaw. After he thwarts the attempt on his life by Kiger Steele, nearly drowning the would-be assassin, Adam becomes filled with an unforgiving contempt and hatred of the white men who had hired Steele. He starts remembering all the injustices he had ever suffered at the hands of white men. His mother, once a slave, had been beaten and raped by her white landlord. When she gave birth to Adam, the landlord refused to acknowledge him, telling her to "keep that little yellow bastard out'a my sight" (266). (Although Adam is genetically half white and half African American he is not thought of by the community as a white man who is half black. Rather, as was then the case with a mixed-race person, he is considered to be an African American who is part white.)

Adam remembers that as a young man, he had been falsely accused of participating in the murder of a white man during a riot. If it had not been for Marcellus Hightower, who later proved his innocence, Adam would have spent his life in prison. The white jurors, who had sent him for life to a prison serving coal mines, had "denied him a human skin" (67). They had looked at him and the other sixteen accused African American men not as individuals but as some evil force that they must destroy.

Recently, Adam had seen that same look on the faces of the landowners in the back room of the lawyer's office.

> They were together against him from the start, but they didn't get mad till he charged out about the county survey-or. Why the hell did he have to do that? Quick as a wink they all froze, froze into one look and he was no longer Adam Atwell to them, but just a nigger who had offended them, white men all together, and they hated him! (55)

Adam resolves to get even with the white men who tried to have him killed. He cannot immediately bring charges against them because he knows that an African American, alone, would receive no justice in the courts against a white banker, lawyer, and several landowners. So he holds Steele prisoner in a nearby town and "puts out" the story that Steele committed suicide because of his troubles with some unnamed white men. When Adam tells his embittered mother of his subsequent meeting with the white men, after their attempt on his life, she congrat-ulates him for outsmarting the white men and making them squirm in their guilt. Together, mother and son relish the sweetness of revenge:

> He sat on in the flickering light, smiling in the fullness of his sense of righteous power, both his temple and his throat pulsing with its thrust in his blood. "Yeah," he said thickly, as if to himself. "They all sit around the table there at the bank, nodding their heads to Adam. I say, 'Kiger jumped in,' And they say, 'He did!' just like they believed it!" Adam laughed brusquely. "They know no nigger goin' to commit suicide! They think I mought've drowned 'im. Least-wise, they hope I did! But they don't dare 'spute my word!" He laughed again contemptuously. "Those low, common, thievin' white mens! Do anythin' for a dollar!" He hawked and spat on the blaze. "They ain't anything too low down for them to do, and they kin git a nigger to do hit for 'em!" (263)

Adam hopes that Mrs. Hightower will bring court action against Oswalt Paley, one of the townsmen whom she discovers masterminded the scheme to defraud her of her clay deposits. If the case goes to court, Adam plans to resurrect Steele as a witness against Paley, hoping that his own case against the other white men will come out during the trial and lead to further prosecutions. However, Mrs. Hightower, who does not know about the attempt on Adam's life, forgives Paley, in a spirit of Christian charity, of his acts against her.

In a dramatic moment at the end of the novel, when Mrs. Hightower tells Adam of her decision not to prosecute Paley, that she has, in fact, returned to him the incriminating evidence that she had planned to use in court, Adam feels thoroughly beaten—ruined. Not only will he lose his cotton land, but he will also never get even with the whites who tried to kill him. For several minutes he loses control of himself, staggers backwards, barraged by images from his past—images of fear and suffering and hatred striking him in the face "like blowing hail" (292).

In this stream of images (one and a half pages long) Cheney reviews all the major scenes in the novel as they pass through Adam's mind. This review helps prepare the reader for Adam's catharsis: "suddenly Adam was standing. . . again, in the clear August morning sun, wringing wet, and limp and weak, standing about twenty steps away from the porch, facing the storehouse. But he knew, without thinking, that he was clean of anger and hate—hate of Paley or anybody else—and he felt within him a mild, sweet buoyancy" (293).

What Adam does not realize at that time is that his defeat is only partial. Though he will have no revenge, he will not, as he thought, lose the Wyche field. Just as Adam remained steadfast in his pledge to protect Mrs. Hightower, so she remained loyal to him and Marse. Because of her insistence on excluding the Wyche field and the clay deposits from the sale, the buyers finally lose interest and leave town to look for land less encumbered.

At the end of the novel, Mrs. Hightower, who "had endured her Georgia exile by the light of her dream of returning to Charleston," is reconciled to staying on her land. "There was to be no Indian summer for her. Her title to *wild land on the banks of the Oconee* had carried an irrevocable commitment! This was Hightower country, father and son, and Marse must grow up in it. Raw, rough, dark land, but somehow it was vital. And not the least of its vitality was in the illiterate mixed negro before her, torn from the womb of sin and slavery and curiously shaped in God's image, the only man alive she had complete confidence in, her son's foster father!" (294).

This is Adam ends with the heroic Adam, a man of immense courage and integrity, having been tested and found insufficient—insufficient because of his race and social position to be a full partner with Mrs. Hightower, and insufficient because of his need for revenge, to rise to the full measure of his heroic nature. Yet these failures are, as those of Ratliff Sutton in *River Rogue*, tempered with the possibility of a new beginning. For Ratliff, it is a new beginning free from pride and ambition; for Adam it is a new beginning free from anger and hatred, and with a renewed sense of responsibility to the Hightower family and the land that binds all of their lives together.

This is Adam was published in the fall of 1958. Even though the sales were modest, the reviews were exceptionally good. Several critics praised Cheney's understanding of Southern life, especially his sensitivity to the relation between the races.

John David Marshal, writing in 1960 for the *Georgia Review* reported:

> The author presents the relationship of White and Negro with understanding and quiet dignity, capturing in this his third novel the subtleties of the etiquette of race relations in the Deep South at the turn of the century. . .His view of the relations between the two races is based on a sure knowledge and appreciation of the South and things Southern, rather than on the sensational and the sociological. (Marshal 117).

Walter Sullivan of Vanderbilt University spoke highly of Cheney's craftsmanship in *This is Adam*:

> It would be hard to praise Mr. Cheney's technical achievement too highly. He is good at creating the South Georgia background; he conveys in depth and sharp detail the sight and smell and feel of the country, the sense of trees and big sky and deep river. His book is flawlessly constructed. The flashbacks are strategically placed and Cheney moves into the past and out of it again with that seemingly effortless grace which is the touch of a master. (Sullivan).

R. R. Purdy, also of Vanderbilt, noted the novel's tragic dimensions:

> The narrative is less concerned with Adam as a symbol of a downtrodden race than with Adam as a human being, struggling against almost insuperable odds to maintain his pride and dignity. . . .Like the tragic protagonists of all great art, Adam can discover the really important things, and come to know himself only through his personal loss and downfall. (Purdy 25).

Ralph McGill, Cheney's old friend from his days as a student and reporter (see Chapter III) and now the editor of the

Atlanta Constitution, personally reviewed *This is Adam* for his readers.

This will be part personal reminiscence and part book review. When I was a young reporter I roomed with another member of the staff. He was a Georgian from Fitzgerald and Lumber City, named Brainard Cheney. We burned to be writers, authors of books and of magazine articles.

And, of course, we talked out of our own lives and experiences. Cheney had, as did I, a rural background. His was one of the great lumber area and of plantation-type farming. One of the characters he remembered best was a Negro farm worker, uneducated, but wise, who had in him the basic essence of man and his best qualities of loyalty, faith, compassion, courage and the stubborn will to endure.

I watched for this man in Cheney's first two novels, "Lightwood" and "River Rogue." Both of these had a South Georgia locale and story. Both grew out of the great lumber operations which for years covered the Altamaha with rafts and brought riches, turbulence, folly, cruelty and ruthlessness in their wake.

But now in the third novel, "This is Adam," comes the character I heard about so often more than 30 years ago. He is called Adam in this excellent novel. It is again a Georgia story.

It seems to me that in the choice of the title, Cheney has made of Adam the symbol of man as William Faulkner discussed him in his magnificent speech accepting the Nobel Prize in literature. Adam is all men. But all that enables man to endure is his faith, his compassion, his love. In *This is Adam*, Adam lives because he has the qualities to endure.

I assuredly recommend it to all who like a good novel with well drawn characters and a plot which reaches a high peak of drama.

And it is good, too, after all these years to find a character well remembered out of cub-reporter days, at last fittingly pictured in a good book. (McGill)

In addition to McGill's kind words about him and his novel in the *Atlanta Constitution*, Cheney was further honored by his home state when the Georgia Writer's Association selected *This is Adam* for its annual "Literary Achievement Award for Fiction."

Quest of the Pelican

In *This is Adam*, Cheney used the issue of race relations in the South as a means to dramatize Adam's heroic qualities: his courage and integrity in spite of his inferior social position and in the face of a hostile, white community. In his next novel, *Quest of the Pelican*, Cheney once again took up the issue of

race, but this time, he approached it directly as his central subject.

For the South, the decade of the 1950s was a turbulent period in race relations. In 1954, Southerners were shocked when
the Supreme Court ruled that racially segregated public schools
were unconstitutional (Adams and Burke 143-145). They felt
that this decision, by an agency of government that knew little
about their situation, was unreasonable; it seemed to demand
of them an immediate solution to a cultural problem that was
as old as the nation itself, one that, because of its complexity,
Southerners had chosen to ignore, one that, in fact, they had
privately feared for years and had hoped they would never have
to face. Confused and frightened, Southerners asked their public officials and legislators to appeal to the courts and to enact
state legislation that would prevent, or at least slow down, racial integration in their schools. When these measures failed,
some became belligerent in their protest, reverting to violence
and civil disorder to prevent what they believed to be federal
encroachment in their lives.

In 1957, Cheney was still working as an aide to Governor
Frank Clement when African Americans began their first sit-ins
in Greensboro, North Carolina, when President Eisenhower

sent federal troops into Little Rock, Arkansas, to enforce the
Supreme Court's ruling and when angry white citizens were
rioting and boycotting desegregated schools in New Orleans,
Louisiana (*Britannica Book of the Year* 126).

In Tennessee, Cheney had seen Governor Clement forced to
use state troops and the National Guard in 1956 when nine African American students attempted to enter an all-white school
in Clinton. Cheney was shocked and outraged when Hattie Cotton Primary School in Nashville was dynamited in 1957 and
when Clinton High School was destroyed by explosives a year
later in October of 1958 (142).

Disturbed by these events, Cheney decided in 1960 to write
a fictional account of what happened in Clinton, to typify what
was occurring in other towns and cities across the South. He
planned to expose, in this sociological novel, what he considered to be the real nature of racial prejudice, its source in the
human psyche, how it operates in a society, how it spawns violence, and what the nation—but more particularly each person—must do to be free of it (Cheney, "To Robert Penn Warren").

When Cheney first conceived *Quest of the Pelican*, he pro-
jected it as the third novel in his trilogy, following *Devil's*

Elbow, which would tell the story of Marse Hightower as a young man. However, Cheney was convinced by the editors at McDowell, Obolensky, his publisher, to write the "desegregation novel" immediately to take advantage of its topicality. One of the unfortunate results of this decision is that the last two novels do not build upon each other. Being written out of sequence, the older Marse Hightower's story is told before the young man's. Both stories, however, do refer to characters and incidents in the foundation novel, *This Is Adam*.

John Casper (in hat), model for Cheney's fictional Sherman LeBlanc, speaking to a crowd in Clinton, Tennessee in 1957. *(Courtesy Nashville Public Library)*

The action of *Quest of the Pelican* begins in 1957. Marse Hightower, who is now middle-aged and employed as an aide to the governor of the state, is sent to the rural community of Sycamore to investigate a disturbing rumor. The governor has been warned that racial trouble may break out when Sycamore's previously all-white schools open under a court order to desegregate. Marse discovers that an outside agitator, Sherman LeBlanc, has been talking with Sycamore's citizens, trying to arouse them to resist the court order.

Though LeBlanc is a bright young man, raised by an affluent New England family and educated at an Ivy League school, he is neither an intellectual nor a social liberal. He is, instead, a rabble rouser, dedicated to fighting racial integration. When Marse and the sheriff stop LeBlanc, he skillfully avoids their questions and challenges them to call a meeting of the town council and school board. At that time, he promises to give them a full account of why he is in Sycamore and what the city officials must do to stop the desegregation of their schools. Marse and the sheriff refuse his request, and the sheriff warns him that he will be arrested if he disturbs the peace. LeBlanc, mockingly, invites them to his Monday night speech on the town square where he plans to take his case to the people.

Marse realizes that LeBlanc is potentially dangerous, but he underestimates this young man's power to stir up people's racial prejudice and repressed hostility. During the Monday night gathering, Marse is stunned at the sight of his fellow citizens, whom he thinks of as reasonable, down-to-earth people, slow to anger and distrustful of strangers, breaking, suddenly and irrationally, into passionate outbursts and riotous shouting by LeBlanc's inflammatory rhetoric:

He began walking about, mopping his face and neck and wrists and unbuttoning his collar. Then he hurried forward and leaned down to the people at the edge of the truck. "I'll tell you this." His voice was conversational, though it carried. "Your school board tells you that they can't keep the Negroes out of your school. They say the United States Supreme Court has ordered them to let the Negroes in and they've got to do it. I'm telling you people of Ford County," he breathed in sweet and deadly confidence, "there is one Court in this country that is higher than the Supreme Court!"

The nervous lips of the toothless old man halted, as he fixed the speaker with his stare. Behind him a sinewy man, built like a firedog, with a double length of neck, threw up his long triangular face intently. A woman with a baby in her arms at the edge of the crowd turned back.

LeBlanc straightened up, seeing that he had them again. "Yes. There's one court in this country higher than the Supreme Court," he repeated and lifting his head in that odd gargling way that I had noted before, he intoned triumphantly, "That great court is the people!"

The applause was sudden and torrential. I was astonished and more surprised when it continued on and on, in successive waves. . . .

They echoed him. "Court's the people!"

Measuring the rhythm, he went on, with equal syllabic emphasis: "We must have no integration in our schools!"

"No integration in our schools!" they returned.

I turned at the sidewalk to look back. The crowd was scattering and at first I thought it was breaking up. I saw then that the youngsters were forming a queue. After a moment they began to snake dance, moving around the courthouse. They were shouting, "Keep the Niggers out!" (Cheney, *Quest of the Pelican* 20-24)

That Monday night meeting is the beginning of a troubled season of social unrest in Sycamore. No one in the community is in favor of the desegregation ruling. Even the leaders of the community—the city officials, school board members, sheriff, and school principal—who support the court order do so not from a belief in desegregation but because the highest court in the land has said that it must be so, and they fear that a defiance of the law will bring violence and civil disorder to their community. Their halfhearted support is not strong enough to offset the influence of LeBlanc. He activates the local KKK and encourages the foundation of several White Citizens groups to protest the court order. He and his followers cause so much havoc in Sycamore that Marse has to ask the governor to send in the state police and the National Guard to protect the African American citizens and to restore order.

In addition to the public drama, Cheney examines, through the character of the intellectual and introspective Marse High-tower, the personal meanings of racial integration. He narrates the story from Marse's first person, retrospective point of view. All the events of the novel are filtered through his sensibility as he tries to grasp their significance. Upset by the violence that he sees, Marse seeks to discover within human nature the root causes of racial feelings. To accomplish this task, he first examines his own past to understand why he supports the ideals of an integrated society; then he investigates the life of Sherman LeBlanc, who represents an opposite view, to find out why Le-Blanc is so bitterly opposed to the mixing of the races.

Marse's sympathy for African Americans arises from his relationship with Adam Atwell, the mixed-race overseer of his mother's plantation. When Marse was a boy, Adam had been a foster father to him; through their friendship, Marse had come to understand and appreciate the problems of the African American citizens. Yet their relationship left Marse with ambivalent feelings about race and identity. On a few occasions in his past, he found himself unexpectedly attracted to women of mixed breeding. These impulses always left him feeling guilty, disturbed, and confused, and he wonders if they are connected with his sense of identity, being perhaps some unconscious movement toward the race of his foster parent, an African-American man.

But what about LeBlanc, Marse asks. What motivates a social agitator? What causes LeBlanc's racial hatred? Marse believes that he will find, in LeBlanc's personal history, the genesis of the sickness of racial prejudice. Learning its cause, he hopes to gain insight into its cure.

During his investigation for the governor, Marse learns that LeBlanc had once lived in Greenwich Village with an attractive mixed-race woman of African descent named Missey Marble. They had been students at New York's City College and were active pro-labor, pro-integration radicals, publishing *Call*, an interracial quarterly. When Missey became pregnant, something snapped in LeBlanc's mind. He felt his sense of identity, his New England white ancestry, threatened by the thought of fathering a 'half-breed' child. He became panicky and insisted on aborting his progeny. When Missey refused, he hit her in the stomach and forced her to an abortionist.

Marse finds all this out as he too becomes involved with Missey Marble. As an assistant editor of an African American journal, *The Amsterdam Avalanche*, she invites him to New York to examine at firsthand what Northern schools are like. Because the governor is interested in the North's handling of the racial problem and because of his interest in LeBlanc's history, Marse accepts her invitation.

Missey escorts him through the schools of Harlem, and Marse sees that the Northern schooling system, under de facto segregation, is just as discriminatory as the Southern system. Missey and Marse have a series of intellectual discussions about desegregation during his visit. He argues that the ideological basis for integration—that it is a move toward equality— is wrong-headed and that another more truthful and more powerful concept, an idea that will serve as a foundation, is needed for peoples of all races to live in social accord. After a night on the town and cocktails, dancing, and discourse, their theoretical arguments about racial equality and Christian love narrow down to a biological resolution: Marse is seduced by this attractive woman.

The next morning he awakens in anguish and remorse:

> I felt myself emerging, awakening, coming to consciousness and I wanted to shrink back into oblivion. . . .
>
> I felt that if I turned my head my neck would break in two. The conscious organism that saw the ceiling at that moment might have been reckoned animal, but scarcely human. And I could not name the compulsion that made me turn fearfully to look. Yet I did, to stare at the half uncovered brown body. . .of the sleeping Missey, for an instant—then, quickly down at my own white shoulder, to sink back on the bed with my eyes shut agonizingly tight and my face an ineradicable knot of pain. Trying to shrink backward, backward, like a crayfish darting into his mud. (269)

Marse quickly leaves Missey's apartment, feeling that he has crossed a forbidden barrier that must be preserved; miscegenation, the act that he unconsciously desired, is not an answer for him. He is convinced that while racial pride, like LeBlanc's and the prejudice that it spawns, must be surrendered, it must be surrendered not to bring about a biological mixing of the races, but surrendered to clean the way for the growth of Christian humility and charity—the only viable foundation for people of both races to live in harmony.

This quick turn of events at the end of the novel leaves readers wondering, "What exactly has Marse learned?" Readers know that Marse now understands that his attraction to integration has had subconscious dimensions, that he believes integration based on an ideology of equality is wrong, and that because of his experience with Missey, he feels that interracial sexual taboos are inexplicably but unquestionably valid. Readers do not know, however, whether Marse is still an integrationist, whether his search for the roots of racial prejudice has convinced him that the races should stay not only sexually separate but socially apart as well. Readers do not, nor can they, project what difference the final episode will make in the private lives of Marse and Missey. Worse still, they no longer care because their concern for these characters has been eclipsed by an ideological resolution.

In a letter to Cheney, Robert Penn Warren praised the novel as an "engrossing narrative, convincing and recognizable. . .I think LeBlanc is very well done, the politicians and townspeople, ditto." But he was sharply critical of the book's resolution:

I am totally unconvinced by the development of the Marse-Missey relationship. What I see is an intellectual construct. I don't see, to be simple, what background we have for her wanting to get Marse into bed. The scene in the show is just no-go, on its own account and as preparation. What is convincing is Marse's next-morning hang-over, physical and spiritual, but not what it leads to.

I don't see, in other words, what the end of the novel stacks up to in relation to trouble in Dixie—and boy, is there trouble. I don't see what on practical grounds the end of the novel tells a black man or a white man in Tennessee to do. It may tell somebody how to feel—but there's more to things than that. (Warren, "To Brainard Cheney")

Later in this same letter, Warren comes even closer to the real difficulty of *Quest of the Pelican*. Speaking again about the novel's conclusion, he says, "I honestly believe that you have to rethink the end, and what you want the end to mean" (Warren, "To Brainard Cheney"). The mysterious "it" that Warren speaks of refers to the formalist's conception of organic unity. This idea holds that the parts of a novel create pressures, tensions, and expectations, and that each new incident or character, taking on a life of its own, demands certain configurations from the following events, saying "No! This scenario is untrue" or "Yes, that one is right."

Cheney's conclusion in *Quest of the Pelican* does not read as if it had passed this organic acid test. Instead, it reads like his "Christian Political Realism's" answer to racism in America. As with his political novel, *The Image and the Cry*, the literary result is, in John Crowe Ransom's terms, an aesthetic mixture: art ostensibly in the service of polemics.

In a letter to playwright Maryat Lee in 1958, Flannery O'Connor remarked that she had a friend in Tennessee who would like to meet James Baldwin, the author. "His name is Brainard Cheney and he is writing a novel set in interracial circles in New York. So last month he took a trip to New York where he has a lot of liberal abolishionist [sic] friends to get them to introduce him to some interracial society. He stayed two weeks and pulled all his strings and wasn't able to meet one Negro socially. Well, at least down here we are benighted over the table not under it. If he comes to New York again, I'll get him to call you and maybe you could scout up a few."

Cheney never found a publisher for his desegregation novel (as he called it). McDowell, Obolensky, the company that had published *This Is Adam* and that encouraged him to write *Quest of the Pelican*, went out of business, leaving Cheney without a publisher. In a letter to Vivienne Koch, Cheney complained, "Three Eastern publishers have returned it with the word that they made no editorial criticism, but just didn't want to try to market it" (Cheney, "To Vivian Koch").

It is likely that in addition to the novel's aesthetic problems, these publishers sensed that the public was too close to the problems depicted in the novel to enjoy reading about them. The 1960s was the decade of attacks by whites on the Freedom Riders in Birmingham, Montgomery, and Jackson; Governor George Wallace's standing in the schoolhouse door to prevent integration in Alabama; and in the latter part of the decade, massive rioting and looting by African American rioters in Harlem, Watts, Newark, and Detroit (Adams and Burke 145-160). Newspapers, with their constant reports of racial strife, were severe enough for the public to cope with, without having to be reminded of these problems in their fiction.

Today, the racial issues that Cheney addressed in *Quest of the Pelican* are only partially resolved and are still potentially dangerous. A racially integrated society based on Christian principles remains an unrealized ideal in American life. But Cheney's attempt to come to grips with, or at least shed light on, the nation's most disturbing social problems is reminiscent of the acts of his fictional characters; though unsuccessful, and perhaps even unwise, the attempt alone was a bold and coura-

geous act.

CHAPTER IX
Devil's Elbow
A Novel of Redemption

The last and most complex work in Cheney's trilogy of novels is *Devil's Elbow*. In this novel, Cheney examines the relationship between time and meaning. He addresses the questions: Are the past, present, and future disjointed and independent segments on a straight line, one in which contemporary man is free from the constraints of the past to build his Brave New World? Or is man inextricably bound in the fabric of time, where the past, present, and future are so interwoven that each act in his life grows out of preceding scenes, shapes future acts, and participates in the total meaning of his life?

Cheney explores these questions of time and meaning in the life of his protagonist, Marcellus Hightower. At the beginning of the novel, Marcellus, who was but a young boy in *This is Ad-*

am, is twenty-six years old and a newspaper reporter in Nashville, Tennessee. As a member of the postwar era, he enthusiastically takes part in the wild, rebellious, and emancipated lifestyle of the "Roaring Twenties." But all is not perfect in the Bohemia of Nashville, for Marcellus is haunted by memories from his past, memories that turn his present life into a limbo and his future into a realm of possibilities stuck in time.

Devil's Elbow is a problem novel that revolves around a task set by Cheney for his hero. Marcellus must face the mysteries of his past and unravel their meanings before his present and future life can become more than aimless wanderings. To do this, he makes four returns to Riverton, Georgia, that structure the novel into four sections.

During the Christmas season of 1926, Marcellus interrupts his Bohemian-styled life to make "The First Return" to Georgia. Through extensive flashbacks, the reader is taken on a journey back in time to the disturbing years of Marcellus's transition from an adolescent to a young man. As he sits for long hours on the train, he remembers a series of tragic events that occurred seven years before in Riverton.

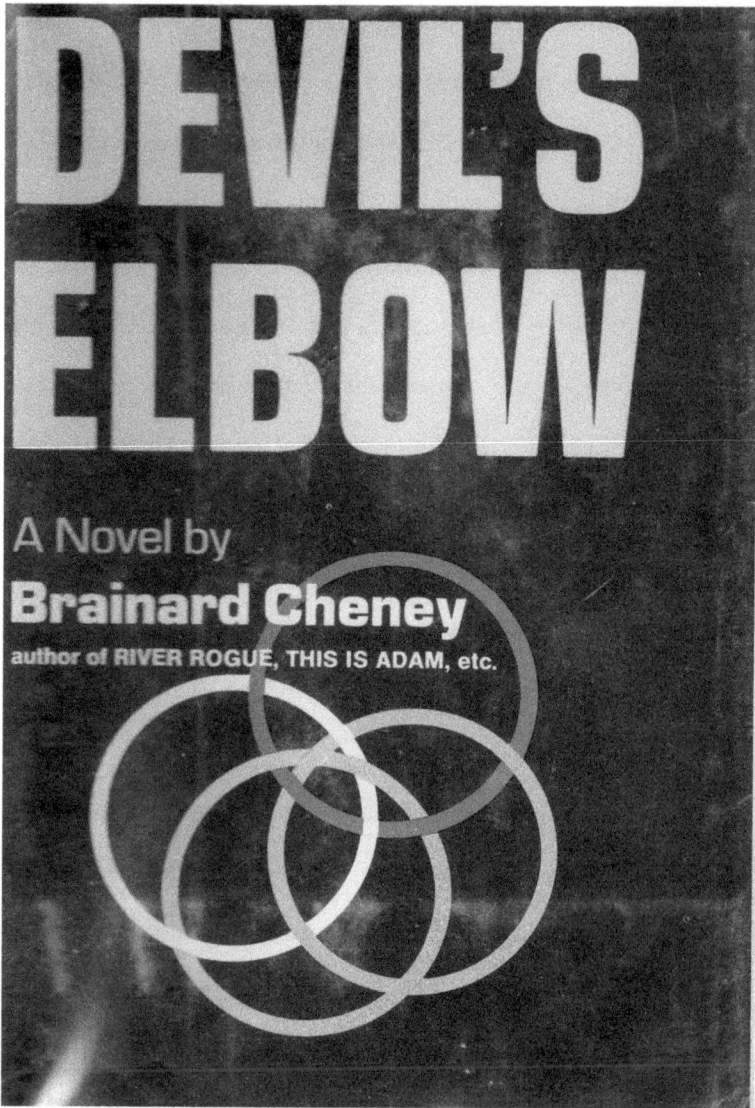

Devil's Elbow appeared in 1969, released by Crown Publishers. It was Cheney's fourth and last published novel.

He was twenty-one years old then and beginning a small lumber enterprise. One Saturday, he asked his best friend, David Ransom, to go out to the old Hightower place to pay off his workers; Marcellus had wanted to travel to surrounding towns that day to buy stumpage for future business. Almost unthinkingly, he suggested to David that he check with Buck Fykes to get in some turkey hunting while he was there. Buck was a disreputable "swamp rat" who lived in the area, hunting and selling illegal "moonshine" whiskey.

David never returned from that hunting trip. The town's sheriff and mayor, as well as David's relatives and friends, conducted a countywide search for him. They caught three suspects who, accusing each other, confessed that David had been killed and that his body had been sunk in the Oconee River. Yet after weeks of dragging the river, no one could find the body. A full six weeks after David had been reported missing, Marcellus, who was hunting on an island in the Oconee River, found the decomposed remains of his friend:

He looked again through the washup of logs and brush on ahead of him at the point of the island, and saw extended crookedly the sleeve of a khaki shirt. His throat went dry, and his breath began to pop out of his mouth as if pistoned by a pump.

In his scramble he lost his hat and almost tore his jacket off him, but at last he leaped upon a log that allowed him to look down on the khaki shirt—to look down on khaki breeches and woods boots, too, covering a blackened and rotting corpse, hung under a freshet-swept sparkleberry bush, face upward.

It was featureless, except for the bared teeth. But he identified it instantly: the boots, the breeches, the shirt, the teeth—it couldn't be anybody but David Ransom! (Cheney 77)

Cheney makes David's murder the central problem of the novel; all the events and characters revolve around it, especially Marcellus, for *Devil's Elbow* is his story. The murder is like a magnet for Marcellus. No matter how hard he tries to forget it, its force is always pulling at him in the periphery of his consciousness. His four returns to Georgia are his attempts to understand his relationship with David, the murder, his complicity, if any, in the murder, and what its implications are for him.

An understanding of Marcellus's relationship with David is central to an understanding of the novel. As Marcellus recalls scenes from his past, the reader learns that he and David had a long and complex friendship. As boys, they were drawn together because they were both fatherless.

David was, above all, the smile that lay in his luminous brown eyes, bearing always in their depths the elusive light that played between merriment and melancholy. [They] had played, fought, studied, courted, and even swapped dreams and ambitions together. (*Devil's Elbow*, 23).

But David slowly grew away from Marcellus. He was older, larger, and came into knowledge of the world quicker and with a fuller understanding than Marcellus.

As young boys, it was David who exhibited courage when he and Marcellus had witnessed the baiting of a young African American houseboy and girl by the Rawlings boys.

Marcellus had heard of boys who played at putting a dog to a bitch in heat. But human beings! His legs began to tremble, and his stomach did a flip. Surely he must be wrong? He turned to David to encounter his own appalled suspicion in David's eyes.

But it was in front, when David swung open the door and called to Jughead to come on out, that Marcellus had turned to stare at David in astonishment and gratitude and had seen that, in spite of the pulse at his throat, he took his time to meet Carver's gaze, and smiled.

His own reaction had been tardy and stiff. And the shame of his cowardice was with him still. Though it hadn't been so much his fear of bodily harm as his fear of the Rawlings boys' ridicule that had paralyzed him. (*Devil's Elbow*, 33)

It was also David who, during their late adolescence, had taken the first step out of boyhood chastity into sexual knowledge, and Marcellus both resented and envied him for it. He condemned him as lustful and irresponsible by the Victorian codes under which they both had been raised, though it was his being deserted, left behind by his friend that had hurt Marcellus the most. Having bridled his sexual stirrings, he secretly envied David's adventures with the opposite sex.

He was especially disturbed by what he thought was David's sexual encounter with Melanie Crosby, a young, but physically mature, friend of David's sister.

As Marcellus came across the back porch to enter the hall, David and Melanie were coming into it from the other end, out of the guest room. David had an arm about her shoulders. And Marcellus could swear, could almost swear that he was playing with one of her breasts—of which she was so proud. But by the time Marcellus got through the screen door, they had separated. Indeed, he was sure David jerked his arm away, when Marcellus took hold of the latch. (*Devil's Elbow*, 99).

Because of Marcellus's own attraction to Melanie, this scene etches itself into his memory, fused in his adolescent mind with feelings of desire, betrayal, and contempt.

When Marcellus first hears about David's death, he is stunned and confused. He asks himself a thousand questions to determine his culpability. He accepts that, though he had no direct responsibility for the tragedy, he had set things in motion that resulted in his friend's death. He had known that the river rat, Buck Fykes, was not to be trusted; he knew that David, in the fullness of his youth, felt himself invulnerable to harm; but though the potential for tragedy dimly floated in Marcellus's awareness, he never openly thought out the possibilities that came about—that David would ask Buck about the turkeys, that he would be invited to drink moonshine liquor from Buck's still, that Buck and his two companions would grow suspicious of him, murder him, and sink his body in the Oconee River.

In a movement away from the central problem of the novel, Marcellus leaves Riverton after his Christmas visit and returns to Nashville, determined to forget the haunting tragedy of his youth. In his flight from the past, Marcellus becomes not only an individual trying to escape his personal history, but Cheney's symbol of twentieth century man adrift in a meaningless world, cut off from the collected wisdom of his culture's past as preserved in its traditions, values, and beliefs.

Embracing a new liberated style of life, Marcellus throws himself into the spirit of the 1920s. He puts behind him all antiquated ideas of morality and ethics, especially the Victorian sexual restrictions of his childhood, to live a full, free, and unencumbered life. One night at a party on the Nashville bluff, overlooking the Cumberland River, Marcellus meets an attractive Nashville co-ed. This young woman, whom he doesn't recognize at first, turns out to be a figure from his past; she is Melanie Crosby, the young girl he had seen seven years ago with David Ransom. She had fully grown up now, moved to Nashville to attend college, and had become, like Marcellus, an enthusiast of the emancipated and carefree Jazz Age. Both Marcellus and Melanie outwardly scorn tradition and bourgeois ideas of manners and respectability, but beneath their display, each is a rather sad figure, heroically struggling against a past that weighs them down.

Although Melanie is a character who never quite comes to life—possibly because she has so little dialogue of her own, most of her actions being reported through the filter of Marcellus's memory—she is nevertheless a central figure, if only symbolic, in the novel. Through her, Cheney can show Marcellus's rejection of tradition, his attitudes toward sex and love, and his dire need to search for a clearer understanding of the tragedy in his past.

Marcellus and Melanie later marry, but without an old-fashioned engagement or a formal church ceremony, and they move into a small apartment where Marcellus continues in his work as a reporter, writing in his spare time short stories that don't sell, while she helps support them by teaching school. Spurning traditional morals and conventions, they impose no sexual restrictions on each other, and over the years, Marcellus, who is always restless and discontented, takes to bed several different women, and Melanie has at least one platonic affair. Eventually, these extra-marital affairs destroy their relationship, and after fourteen years of marriage, they separate.

The title, *Devil's Elbow*, refers to a bend in the Oconee River, where raftsmen who used to float timber down the river had to be especially careful. The river picked up speed in the elbow and rafts were often destroyed in its swirling crosscurrents. In the novel, Marcellus is caught in a type of Devil's Elbow, for he is stuck in the river of time, unable to move into a meaningful future.

The wave of movement away from the past is reversed in the last half of *Devil's Elbow*. Cheney once again has his hero return to Georgia to confront his past. Marcellus, now middle-aged, tired, and disillusioned with his free-styled life, returns to Riverton and slowly begins to piece together the full meaning of his friend's death and how it has affected his life.

What he discovers is that though David, in his late adolescence, was beginning to have amorous adventures, they were not as numerous or as cavalier as Marcellus had thought. David had given his fraternity badge to a common girl, not to seduce her as Marcellus imagined, but because the girl had asked him for it to make the man she wanted to marry jealous. Marcellus also finds out that David had not taken advantage of the young Melanie. Their affair was nothing more than a young girl's crush on an older boy.

David possessed an old-fashioned gallantry in affairs of the heart that escaped Marcellus's understanding. In contrast to David, Marcellus's sexual awakening had not been tempered with love, humility, or respect. In his disillusionment with and misunderstanding of David's behavior and in the rebellious casting off of his own sexual inhibitions, Marcellus had come to look upon romantic love with contempt. Relations between men and women were merely biological necessities, and love was for the naïve, sentimental, and adolescent; cynicism and irony were the proper attitudes of a mature man.

Yet for fourteen years of his adult married life, this attitude had brought him no contentment. Marcellus exhibited not only a lack of respect for women and love but also for life itself. After years of protesting to Melanie that he wanted no children, even once intimidating her into having an abortion, he had in the last years of their marriage changed his mind. In a vain attempt at adding stability and worth to his life, he had decided he wanted a child; in fact, he demanded a child from the distraught Melanie. As if life were paying him back for his years of contempt, Melanie could no longer conceive.

Toward the end of the novel, the central problem—the mystery of David's death—comes back to haunt Marcellus with increasing intensity. Though he is separated from Melanie, he is still determined to have a child, even if it means using a woman out of wedlock to produce an offspring for him. However, each time he attempts a seduction, the nauseating smell of David's decaying body revisits him. It comes on him with the same force in which it engulfed him the day he discovered the body. On that day:

> It came over him what this precipitously, perilously, horribly suspended thing was. It was an odor. The sickeningly sweet, ghostly thin, insidiously penetrating smell of rotting human flesh. He had never known it before, but there was no denying it now, for he was saturated with it, from nose to bung. It seeped into the marrow of his bones. His eyes watered of it.
>
> He did not feel fright; he felt an overwhelming horror. David's voice, David's smile, David's eyes; their joking, their fighting, their laughter, their sweat, their whole past, all was consumed in that evil, ineffable smell. (Devil's Elbow, 78-79)

As a narrative device, the haunting, fury-like odor functions perfectly. Through it, Cheney shows that Marcellus's subconscious mind, like nature itself, cannot be defrauded; it will have its say. Not only does the odor thwart Marcellus in his insolent design to bring a new life into the world, but it also forces him into a final confrontation with his past. It forces him to face the fact that he never fully admitted nor forgave himself for his complicity in David's murder.

In an excellent scene Cheney visits Adam Atwell, friend and former land overseer of the Hightower family, who helps Mar-

cellus face the meaning of the tragedy. It is an encounter between age and youth: the distraught prodigal returning, coming
home, to seek understanding.

Adam nodded, then studied the ground, marking on its
hard surface with a lightwood splinter. "Your wife, she never did have a child, did she?" he said, after a time. Marcellus
bridled, but Adam didn't look up. "I-I mean, in no way—
dead, too soon, or anything?"

Marcellus shrugged, then, collecting himself, cleared his
throat. "That's right, she—we never had any." After a pause,
he added ironically, "We were too smart."

Adam agreed, without raising up. "Too smart—then too
late when you changed your mind. Mind," he repeated, "and
got too set on it—I seen that in you four years ago."

"But, Goddamnit, Adam, what's that got to do with David Ransom?" Marcellus exploded. "And this is a real smell,
in my head—in my nose."

His jaw moved abruptly as he jerked his head about, and
his mouth twisted to skeet an arc of tobacco juice at a distant doodle hole. "You don't still think David died for nothing, do you, Marcellus?"

Marcellus was breathing quick, grimacing, staring like a
man about to be overtaken. He swallowed hard, and his
voice rose in a wavering falsetto as he spoke. "But,
Goddamnit, Adam, what's that got to do with women—or
having children, either?" a tic came in his left cheek, and he
brusquely wiped his mouth. "And after all, Adam, God

knows, we didn't mean David any harm. And it was, was almost, almost a quarter of a century ago! I scarcely remember what he looked like—I—" Marcellus broke off moodily.

"You thinks you forgit, when you just disremember!" Light shimmered in Adam's eyes; then he lifted the lightwood splinter, unlit but potent. "Hit's dere, deep. . . Hit's dere. And hit all add up, all add together."

Marcellus jumped to his feet, scrounging his shoulders up and the back of his head down against them, stamping in protest, circling about. "But, Adam, it don't add up! This is a smell in my head! Broken off somehow—broken off—" He shrugged in frustration, still circling. "It can't be wrong for a man to want children!". . .

"You think that smell's broke off in your head—that it don't make no sense—just aimless and got twixt you and your nature—that it can't be wrong for a cold-codded man like you to have children!. . .Anything can be wrong in this world, son—almost—can be different from what you think it is. Like that smell being in your head, you think". . . .

"Hit's not in your nose, Marcellus, no neither in your head. Hit's in your heart!"

Marcellus had seen it coming: those last four words, had known how Adam would put it. Still, when they came, they went through him like a swallow of fire just the same, and he couldn't check himself. He got out his handkerchief and wiped his eyes. He stood up, too. He stamped on the ground to wake up his right leg. He spoke in a chastened voice. "All right, Adam—I guess I had to have *you* tell me!" (*Devil's Elbow*, 237-239, 242)

In the resolution of *Devil's Elbow*, Marcellus finally solves the problem of the novel; he sees, as a whole, the pattern of his relationship with David Ransom and what it has meant in his life. He realizes that he had been jealous of David's courage and manliness and that he had resented being left behind in his adolescent naivety when David became interested in the opposite sex. When this resentment became linked with his sexual awakening, it had turned into hostility; subconsciously, he had wanted David out of the way, much as a son wants to displace his father or his older brother. Marcellus further understands that he had not displaced the real David. Instead, he had corrupted the memory of his friend, making him seem wanton and irresponsible to justify his sexual liberation. But David's natural goodness, his charm, grace, and gallantry had outlived Marcellus's scorn.

In Marcellus's mind David takes on the qualities of Christ, and he sees himself as, if not a Judas, then a contrite sinner. In the following passage, the name of Christ could easily be substituted for David's:

David was dead. But David lived, too—daily. It went back. . . to the fatherless beginning they faced together. It wasn't their intention, but David had laid it all on the line for him. . .For a time his vindictive suspicion had discredited that gaze, had—he thought—put David in the past. But David lived with him, and it was never past. What Marcellus saw now, sitting there below the blue haze of tobacco smoke, was that the eyes could ask things of him, too. He could not live at ease with himself without David's regard— and more. (*Devil's Elbow*, 244)

After Marcellus accepts his guilt, forgives himself, as best he can, and learns that he must have David's respect, his feelings about himself and his relationship with Melanie change. "He had learned some things, though the learning came hard. He saw where he was. And he knew finally what he wanted" (*Devil's Elbow*, 243).

He learns that the present and future are, rather than escapes from the past, fulfillments of it, and the mature love is never free; in order to exist, it must be based on trust, responsibility and commitment.

However, lightly and provisionally, he may have entered into it, he made a commitment to her, fifteen years ago. They made a commitment. It was hard to say how such commitments were made or what sealed them. How? Wasn't it really a part of the heedless act itself—the meaning time discovers in the thing essentially mindless, but living; because it lives? And, in right and wrong, hadn't they built on it? Perhaps it would be better to say that it—the commitment—had built on them. (*Devil's Elbow*, 244-245)

At the end of the novel, he and Melanie are reunited. They realize that they are bound to each other by their pasts, that "their fulfillment still lay in their marriage and through it," (244-245) and that though they could not bring life into the world, they could go out of life together (247).

In his continuing interest in the insufficient hero, Cheney creates in Marcellus Hightower the least heroic of his central characters. Compared to Micajah Corn, Ratliff Sutton, and Adam Atwell, Marcellus seems small, indeed. Nor is he a protagonist that attracts much sympathy from the reader.

In appraising an early draft of *Devil's Elbow*, a book reviewer for Crown Publishers said, "As for the hero himself he accepts no responsibility for the various abortions, marital and otherwise, that are scattered through his love affairs." Correcting herself, she goes on to say parenthetically: "(Yes, he does say, p. 207, 'He was beginning to suspect that maybe he was just a trifling son-of-a-bitch,' which this reader had suspected from the start)" (W.W.).

Yet there is something heroic about Marcellus. The reader can never quite write him off. Like Gatsby in Fitzgerald's *The*

Great Gatsby, a man who because of his romantic sensibilities remains higher in the reader's esteem than his ways of making a living justify, Marcellus, also, is raised up, not for his romanticism, for that was the first thing he abandoned after his revolt from Victorian morals, but raised up through the earnestness, the agony, of his struggle to understand himself. In the midst of his drunkenness or debauchery, he is always haunted by his acts, by his past, and by his lack of understanding. He suffers all the ailments of contemporary man who has lost his soul. He lives in a world of guilt, personal suffering, and existential meaninglessness. Marcellus's long and painful struggle, his search for meaning, is a purifying ordeal that ennobles his life and raises his character to the stature of the heroic.

What Marcellus learns in *Devil's Elbow* is what Cheney believes contemporary man must come to know:

That respect for the eternal verities—love, honor, truth, courage—and the cultural traditions and religious beliefs that embody them are absolute requirements for a meaningful life. Without a sense of responsibility to our fellow human beings, without an understanding of how the past participates in the present, without a feeling of humility and respect for life, man is condemned to drift, aimlessly and painfully, through his days.

CHAPTER X
The Search for a Hero

> "Perhaps some of us have to go through dark and devious ways before we
> can find the river of peace or the highroad to the soul's destination."
> — Joseph Campbell, *The Hero With a Thousand Faces*

Though all of Cheney's published novels, *Lightwood, River Rogue, This is Adam* and *Devil's Elbow*, are vastly different—stretching across Georgia history from 1874 to 1945, and with a cast of characters ranging from land squatters and raftsmen to timber barons, plantation owners, reporters, and politicians—a common thematic thread runs through them all, and all their protagonists, about whom the stories revolve, share important similarities.

The main characters of Cheney's fiction—Micajah Corn, Ratliff Sutton, Adam Atwell, and Marcellus Hightower—

possess heroic qualities, traits of character that raise them above the common lot of man and that give their stories an aura of intensity and significance. Micajah Corn in *Lightwood* is an archetypical American frontiersman, with all the heroic qualities—courage, cunning, strength, prowess—that survival in a Georgia wilderness demands. Ratliff Sutton in *River Rogue*, deprived of honor and respectability in early life, develops an Olympian drive for power that propels him from the lowest social level of river life, a runaway boy living with African American people, to honor among rivermen as a courageous and inventive raftsman, to timber baron among the aristocrats of Darien, Georgia.

Though Adam Atwell, in *This is Adam*, is a person of mixed-race, an overseer on a small plantation in Georgia in a time of fierce prejudice, he possesses an uncommon sense of personal honor and integrity. Standing alone against a hostile white community, remaining true to his promises to a dying man, and wrestling with his own embittered past, Adam exemplifies some of man's best qualities. Even Marcellus Hightower in *Devil's Elbow*, though not a typical hero, has qualities that raise him above the norm. As a contemporary man living in the abyss of existential meaninglessness, his struggle and suffering are so intense that his life and character also share the aura of the heroic.

Yet despite these heroic qualities in Micajah, Ratliff, Adam, and Marcellus, they all possess flaws that make them insufficient to meet the challenges of life. All their successes are partial and transient. Life, meeting the insufficient hero, breaks him and washes away his brief victories in the waves of fate and time. Micajah's pride, his determination to kill Zenas Fears, his cursing God and fate, and the corruption of his sons and daughters that takes place over the long years of their fight with the Northern lumber companies undermine his strength of character and the purity of his struggle. These flaws lead to his downfall. From proud frontier patriarch, he falls before the onrush of Northern industrialism to lowly squatter—humble, broken, and dispossessed of his land.

Ratliff Sutton's fall comes from his blinding drive for power. His struggle for respectability is so intense that he forsakes his friends and loses his sense of himself. At the height of his success, he falls victim to a devastating tragedy, the murder of his wife by his oldest friend. This act of fate leaves him crushed, humbled, and alone. And Adam Atwell, the most nearly sufficient of Cheney's heroes, is also found inadequate. Not only because he is part African American, poor, and uneducated is he not equal to the demands of life but also because he harbors hate, resentment, and a driving need to wreak revenge on the corrupt whites of Riverton who tried to have him killed.

Marcellus Hightower, the young boy whom Adam looked after and cared for in *This is Adam*, grows to young adulthood and rejects both his mother's and Adam's moral codes and values. In *Devil's Elbow*, Marcellus is clearly inadequate for life. Aimlessly adrift in the moral and ethical quagmire of "the lost generation," he is a man who has nothing to stand up to life with. Cut off from his past, the attitudes and values that sustained his ancestors, he rambles through life, thinking himself free of his acts and his responsibilities to others, yet eventually finding that life extracts high payments for such attitudes. He meets confusion and disillusionment in each sexual affair, and despite his efforts to bring a child into the world, life revengefully withholds its blessing.

The fictional worlds that Cheney creates in *Lightwood*, *River Rogue*, *This is Adam*, and *Devil's Elbow* are moral battlefields. The characters with their armory of heroic, nearly superhuman qualities of character, face and do battle with life. Life asks, rather it demands, from these heroes that they be courageous, valiant, responsible, resourceful, and resilient. Otherwise, they will be crushed, for life or fate or nature can cause Zenas Fear's horse to jerk the moment before Micajah's avenging shot is fired. It can cause a hurricane so ferocious that it dwarfs the puny efforts of lumber companies to hold their timber at dock, making and breaking the fortunes of men in a single stroke. Or it can suddenly flood a river with rainwater, leading the ambitious and disrespectful Ratliff into a tragic accident that destroys his raft and kills his boyhood friend. It can also snuff out the life of Micajah's sons, take Ratliff's wife from him, and deny to any man, like Marcellus, the promise of children. Life in Cheney's novels is indeed a fierce adversary.

In the contest of wills with life, all of Cheney's heroes are found to be insufficient. Each in turn is broken by the course of events, and the breaking is nearly always apoplectic and cathartic: In *Lightwood* as Micajah raises a hammer to the sky to curse God, "He threw the hammer from him. He felt his palm tingle as the handle left it. Then the tingling spread, up into his neck. There was a prickling in his right cheek. He looked down and saw that his right arm was hanging by his side. There was a prickling in his leg. He was falling to the ground" (340). Ratliff, in *River Rogue*, is similarly stunned and confounded when he learns of his wife's death, and for days, he stumbles about, groping for an understanding of what has happened and why. "The numbness of shock had partly gone and feeling had returned to his emotional being—and with its pain a pervading, an awesome sense of punishment" (441).

When Adam, in *This Is Adam*, hears from Mrs. Hightower that she will not prosecute the whites of Riverton, he stumbles backward, dazed —"fragments of painful images hit him in the face, like blowing hail—as he moved toward bodily explosion" (282). And when, in *Devil's Elbow*, Marcellus realized his complicity in his friend's death, he downed a quart of whiskey and "sucked in his breath with a long quivering moan and began to heave" (198).

The common theme that runs through all of Cheney's novels, his statement about human nature and man's relation to life, is that all men, even the best of men, the most heroic of our species—the courageous Micajah, the powerful Ratliff, the responsible Adam, and the emancipated Marcellus—all are insufficient to conquer life; all will be eventually broken. Neither courage nor cunning nor intellect nor power can conquer life, for life is but the manifestation of the will of God. God works his awesome way through the histories of nations and the lives of men. He is the force behind nature—the creator and destroyer of life.

In the resolving scenes of Cheney's novels, after the hero's will has been broken, he learns through his suffering that the proper attitude of man to such a power is not one of pride and boastfulness but one of a Christ-like humility and acquiescence to a higher power. In Cheney's fiction, Christianity forms the underlying mythos, with Christ as the last and only truly sufficient hero. The way "to be in the world" is to be like Christ.

After Micajah's stroke, which breaks his pride, he "knew without reflection that God had struck him down. God never held with killing, and he had harbored it in his heart then for ten years . . . Micajah had agreed to forgive his enemies. . . [He] could have no peace until he did God's will" (347). The death of Ratliff's wife brings him to the realization that "Power is not enough . . .You broke your bonds with everyone—and self, blind self swallowed you . . . . Selfishness becomes greed and hate, then turned loose. And greed and hate have no heart, no shame—they keep no faith with man or God. They eat up a man's integrity" (441).

After Adam's dramatic catharsis in the front yard of the Hightower home, he finds himself "standing on the ground again, in the clear August morning sun, wringing wet, and limp and weak . . . He knew, without thinking that he was clean of anger and hate . . . and he felt within him a mild, sweet buoyancy . . . He mused . . . there are more important things [in life] . . . one of 'em's God's freedom" (7). And in *Devil's Elbow*, Adam helps Marcellus see the Christian significance of David Ransom's death:

> "They say the g-good die young." He spoke from the wine-house step, leaning over his knees meditatively. "And always, us h-helps to do 'em in. Just us ordinary, selfish, 'ceitful, arrogant, heedless, sorry sons a bitches." His guttural bass gave pulse to the gloaming. "Sometimes 'e lets a good man to be took out of the tangle of things. Maybe it looks like 'e cuts 'im off. But it ain't so. It ain't never blind. Hit for us. H-Hit done to show us up, to show our own meanness to us. . .and our needs." (198-199)

Later, Marcellus affirms this symbolic connection between David and Christ—"David was dead. But David lived, too—daily . . . He could not live at ease with himself, without David's regard . . ." (244).

Cheney's novels dramatize man's attempt to struggle against the will of God. Each protagonist, asserting his will to the utmost, puffed up in the pride of his heroic qualities, ultimately falls, is broken in climactic scenes that humble him and clear the way for him to have a new vision of his relationship to life. Each hero at the novel's end starts his life again—this time with more humility, with not a struggle of his will against God's but with a Christ-like acceptance that says "Not my will but thine be done."

Micajah, crippled and broken, submits to the will of God, even if it means, as it does for the Old Testament Job, that all his lands will be taken from him. Ratliff turns his back on the empire that he acquired and returns to a simpler life on the rivers of his youth. Adam and Marcellus also begin new lives: Adam, free from hate and his need for revenge, and Marcellus, free from guilt and an empty life. He is free because, as he tells Melanie, "the murdered hero burdens his followers with the crime . . . It's their way to salvation" (255).

Cheney's vision of the nature of the world as exemplified in his novels came about through a personal struggle that spanned over half a century. Since his boyhood days in south Georgia through his life as a student and reporter, politician, novelist, and polemicist, he tried to understand the fundamental nature of man and his proper relationship with the world. Cheney's spiritual and intellectual development formed a pat-

tern not unlike an archetype described by Edward Edinger, a
Neo-Jungian scholar. Edinger writes that in the first half of life
the ego, seeking individuation, often breaks away from the Self
(God, authority, the cultural past) only to return in the second
half of life to the Self, seeking unity and wholeness (5).

At first, Cheney rejected the ideals of his Victorian boyhood
and embraced the optimism of the early twentieth century. His
readings in philosophy, religion, and politics convinced him
that the world was about to enter a great new era, free from
outmoded traditions, free from religion, and free from economic deprivation. A new utopia, he thought, was approaching, a
world where man with his unique gifts of intelligence and will
could create, with the help of science and technology, a new,
more enlightened world.

As Cheney grew older and as his experience with the world
broadened, he began to recognize the limits of the human mind
and the human heart. He saw as a reporter and political aide in
Tennessee and Washington that men were often led not by high
ideals but by egotistic goals. Over the years, his faith in the essential goodness of human nature waned into pessimism, and
his political outlook became firmly conservative. His pessimism
was tempered, however, by an awakening to the spiritual di-

mensions of life and by his conversion in 1953 to Catholicism. He thought that although earthly utopias were foolish and un- realistic, man was not without hope:

> . . . this dimension of human life called direction, under Christianity, proposes to lead a man from ego ob- session to the love of his fellow man for the love of God and by way of grace to self-transcendence and eventual union with God—that is, the Beatific Vision. And it should be added, by this Way, transcendence of death, too—transcendence of time and space, in eternity (Cheney, "To Dick Beatty" June 1961).

Belief in God and redemption through Jesus Christ became the most fundamental ground of Cheney's mental and spiritual life, and it is little wonder that his fiction reflects these con- cerns. Yet in the expression of this Christian ethos, Cheney also recreates a vast range of Georgia history, preserving for the reader a people and a way of life on the great rivers of Geor- gia—the Ocmulgee, the Oconee, and the Altamaha—that have long since vanished into the past. In an article in the *Southern Review*, Cheney wrote, "Scattered over thirty years, in four novels I have sought to celebrate the story of the Altamaha and its people" (156).

His old friend and literary mentor, Caroline Gordon, said of his fiction—"He writes about the backwoodsmen of Southern Georgia because he knows and loves them and he tells us things about them—and mankind in general—that no other writer tells us" (330).

Three times, Cheney let his ideology overshadow the art of his stories. His political novel *The Image and the Cry*, his play, *Strangers in This World*, and his sociological novel, *Quest of the Pelican*, all labor under the weight of his religious conviction. But in his published novels, *Lightwood, River Rogue, This is Adam*, and *Devil's Elbow*, he was able to achieve an artistic synthesis between religious motif and story. In these stories, Cheney's gift for realistic detail—the language, dress, and behavior of land squatters, rivermen, African Americans, and Southern gentry—helped him create compelling characters and believable stories.

The inadequate heroes that he portrayed remain alive in the reader's imagination, long after their stories have been told. Their fierce individualism, their heroic struggles, and their ultimate falls evoke a strong sympathy. When life humbles these insufficient heroes, the reader also feels humbled and led, like the broken hero, toward an acceptance of a new vision. After finishing a Cheney novel, the reader feels: Yes, it is a moral world, and yes, there is a power beyond it greater than our own, a power with which each person—like Micajah and Ratliff, Adam and Marcellus—must ultimately come to terms.

Afterword

After studying Brainard Cheney's life for two years as a Ph.D. candidate of Peabody College of Vanderbilt University, I came into a deep appreciation of the relationship between literature and the life of authors. Through reading all of the Cheney papers in the Special Collections Department of the Jean and Alexander Heard Library and conducting over 50 hours of personal interviews with Cheney at his home, Idler's Retreat, in Smyrna, Tennessee, I began to see how novels and literary essays come into being out of the fabric of a writer's life and culture.

I saw how Cheney worked, how he drafted the first expressions of his novels and essays from his experiences and concerns, how he sent the drafts to friends for review, how those early attempts were reworked into polished prose, and sent to editors, were then published, reviewed, and critiqued by news-papers, magazines, and academic journals and celebrated by his close literary friends.

I began to see Cheney as a mirror and reflector of the forces that had shaped his personal history and the history of the South, and I saw how he contributed to that cultural force by his ardent desire to set forth in works of fiction and essays his experiences and interpretation of human existence.

What impresses the modern reader about Brainard Cheney is the enormous scope and complexity of his life. Like the questing hero Joseph Campbell describes in the *Hero with a Thousand Faces*, the hero that ventures forth out of compla-cency into the world and through adventures and suffering dis-covers truths, insights, and skills that he brings back for the benefit of his community, Cheney set out from his privileged early childhood in rural Georgia to experience life to the fullest as he searched for the meaning and purpose of human exist-ence.

His first task as a young man was to become educated through his private readings of the classics of the western world and attending some of the best colleges and universities of the South. His second task as a political reporter for the *Nashville*

Banner was to study life and politics in Tennessee. As a speechwriter and public relations director for Senator Tom Stewart and Governor Frank Clement, he was able to expand his understanding and influence by participating in national politics, helping to shape public policies on the Tennessee Valley Authority and Civil Rights in Tennessee.

As a novelist, his final task was to share what he had discovered about life by capturing for posterity the life, times, and folkways of rural Georgia from 1874 to 1945. As an essayist in thirty articles published in prestigious Southern academic, literary and scholarly journals, he was able to articulate his findings on religion, politics, and literature, and finally through his extensive correspondence with his contemporary artists and writers, he was able to help us see the richly textured lives and relationships of a community of Southern writers.

Perhaps it could be argued that Cheney's search for a hero that stretched over 89 years of the Twentieth Century was not fully resolved in the lives of his fictional protagonists nor even in the life of Christ and the doctrines of Christianity, in which he so fervently believed, but resolved instead in the fabric of his own life. Cheney himself, through the arc of his dramatic and complex life, was unknowingly the ultimate hero that he had searched for all his life. As T. S. Eliot in the *Four Quartets* said, "We shall not cease from exploration/And the end of all our exploring/Will be to arrive where we started/And know the place for the first time."

When I last saw Brainard Cheney in the summer of 1979, he was in good health and living a vigorous life. At age seventy-nine, he followed a rigorous daily work schedule: Up by six in the morning, he started his day with thirteen laps (one quarter mile) in his private swimming pool; he breakfasted at 8:00 and worked in his study from 9:00 to 1:00. After lunch, he returned for another three or four hours of writing, ending the day with a vigorous swim in the late afternoon. His regimen of work was interrupted only by occasional drives in the countryside that helped him think through difficult ideas or by work in his garden in the spring. As a devout Catholic, each day of Cheney's life was begun and concluded with prayers for the sick and for the souls of his friends who were no longer living.

In the last decade of his life from 1980 to his death on January 15, 1990, in Nashville, as Cheney worked on a fictional biography of his mother's life that he intended to title *Kitty Mood's Cup*, he witnessed a resurgence of interest in his novels. In 1982, Dr. Delma Presley, a Georgia historian, created, under the auspices of Georgia Southern University, Project RAFT (Restoring Altamaha Folk Traditions) which celebrated the life of 19th century Georgia rivermen. These hardy raftsmen cut timber from the pine barrens of south central Georgia, constructed 85 foot long rafts of pine logs and floated them 150 miles down the Altamaha River from Lumber City to the timber markets on the coast at Darien, Georgia. Because Cheney had written about these men in his 1942 novel, *River Rogue*, he was invited as an honored guest to attend the festival, join the reenactment, and deliver talks about the life of the rivermen on the Altamaha River. Project RAFT initiated a documentary, *River of Memories*, by Georgia Public Television, and The Burr Oak company re-published two of Cheney's historical novels about the region: *River Rogue* in 1982 and *Lightwood* in 1984.

In the past five years because of a renewed interest in the history of South Georgia and due to the efforts of Stephen Whigham, former librarian, and Roy Neel, Cheney's nephew and literary executor, all of Cheney's novels have been republished as part of the "Lightwood History Collection" by MMJW BookHouse. All are now available in hardcover, softcover, and eBook formats.

In November of 2016, Cheney was honored posthumously by being inducted into the Georgia Writer's Hall of Fame for his contribution to Southern Literature and the rich literary heritage of Georgia.

Brainard Cheney at Idler's Retreat, late 1970s. *(Courtesy Mary Williams)*

As a novelist, reporter, and polemicist, Brainard Cheney helped the people of Georgia and the readers of Southern literature understand their history, traditions, and role in the development of the contemporary South. It could be said that he sang the song of the Southern people in all their glory, anguish, failures and triumphs, and his song not only helped him understand his part in this large unfolding drama but also helped the South come to terms with its own heroic past. Perhaps the South was the ultimate hero of Cheney' life.

BIBLIOGRAPHY

Part I.   Primary Sources including Works by Brainard Cheney

Manuscript Collections

The papers of Brainard Cheney were collected in 1972 by the Special Collections Department of the Jean and Alexander Heard Library of Vanderbilt University, Nashville, Tennessee. They include the following:

> Drafts and notes of stories, novels, and
> literary articles
> Manuscripts of ghost-written speeches for Governor
> Frank Clement and Senator Tom Stewart
> Scrapbooks of newspaper clippings, letters from pub-
> lishers, and book reviews
> *Nashville Banner* clippings of the voyage of Adventurer
> II, in which Cheney retraced the river route
> taken by early settlers of Nashville

Correspondence, over two thousand letters, including
letters from:

Cleanth Brooks (6 letters)

Donald Davidson (8 letters)

Caroline Gordon (125 letters)

Andrew Lytle (71 letters)

Flannery O'Connor (113 letters)

Allen Tate (43 letters)

Robert Penn Warren (74 letters)

Manuscripts of four published novels: *Lightwood,
River Rogue, This is Adam,* and *Devil's Elbow*

Manuscripts of three unpublished novels: *The Image
and the Cry, Quest for the Pelican,* and *World
Beyond Words.*

Manuscripts of two plays that were produced by the
Vanderbilt University Theater: *Strangers in
this World* and *I Choose to Die*

Published Works of Brainard Cheney

Novels:

Lightwood. Boston: Houghton Mifflin Company,
1939. Also reprinted in a condensed form in
Scribner's Commentary, November, 1939,
December 1939, and January 1940. Repub-

lished in 1984 by Burr Oak Publishers and in 2012 by MM John Welda BookHouse.

River Rogue. Boston: Houghton Mifflin Company, 1942. Republished in 1984 by Burr Oak Publishers and in 2012 by MM John Welda BookHouse.

This is Adam. New York: McDowell, Obolensky, 1958. Republished in 2013 by MM John Welda BookHouse.

Devil's Elbow. New York: Crown Publishers, Inc. 1969. Republished in 2013 by MM John Welda BookHouse.

Short Stories:

"Get on Board Little Children." *Sewanee Review*, 76 (Fall 1968), 437-447.

"Poss." In *A Vanderbilt Miscellany 1919-1944.* Ed. Richmond Croom Beatty. Nashville: Vanderbilt University Press, 1944.

"The Yellow Dress." In *Contemporary Southern Prose.* Ed. Richard Croom Beatty. Boston: D. C. Heath and Co., 1940.

"Thrills of an Ambush in a Georgia Swamp." *Atlanta Constitution*, 26 November 1939. A newspaper sketch.

"To Kill a Bear." *Southern Review*, 75 (July 1974), 671-
685.

"Travel DeLuxe: The Lumber Raft Way." *Atlanta
Journal*, 5 December 1940, p. 14. A newspaper
sketch.

Political and Religious Articles:

"Address to the International Council for Christian
Leadership." Speaker: Governor Frank G.
Clement. Washington D.C., 3 February 1955.
Written by Brainard Cheney, Cheney Papers,
Special Collections Department of the Jean
and Alexander Heard Library of Vanderbilt
University.

"Christianity and the Tragic Vision—Utopianism
U.S.A." *Sewanee Review*, 69 (Fall 1961), 515-
533.

"Conservative Course by Celestial Navigation." *Sewanee Review*, 62 (January 1954), 151-159.

"The Crocodile or the Crucifix: The Politics of Syncretism, Toynbeeism, and Revelation." *Sewanee
Review*, 66 (Summer 1958), 507-518.

"Has Teilhard de Chardin Really Joined the Within and
the Without of Things?" *Sewanee Review*, 73
(Spring 1965), 217-236.

"Howard Johnson's Meals for Millions." *Coronet*, 34
(May 1953), 74-78.

"The Leader Follows—Where?" *Georgia Review*, 2 (Spring 1948).

"A New 'Crown of Thorns' for the Democratic Party." Speaker: Governor Frank G. Clement. Democratic National Convention, Chicago, 1956. Partially written by Brainard Cheney, Cheney Papers, Special Collections Department of the Jean and Alexander Heard Library of Vanderbilt University.

"The Small Business Situation." Speaker: U.S. Senator Tom Stewart. United States Senate, Washington D.C., 22 February 1943. Written by Brainard Cheney, Cheney Papers, Special Collections Department of the Jean and Alexander Heard Library of Vanderbilt University.

"Uncertainty of Survival: Cradle of Consciousness?" *Thought*, 51 (December 1976), 378-392. Co-authored with biologist Antonio M. Gotto.

Literary Articles:

"Can Julia Peterkin's 'Genius' Be Revised for Today's Black 'Myth Making'?" *Sewanee Review*, 80 (1972), 173-179.

"Caroline Gordon's *The Malefactors*." In *Rediscoveries*. Ed. David Madden. New York: Crown Publishers, 1971. Reprinted from *Sewanee Review*, 79 (1971), 360-372.

"Caroline Gordon's Ontological Quest." *Renascence,* 16 (Fall 1963), 3-12.

"Donald Davidson." *Sewanee Review,* 76 (Fall 1968), 691-693.

"Flannery O'Connor's Campaign for Her Country." *Sewanee Review,* 72 (Autumn 1964), 555-558.

"Look-a, Look-a Yonder—I See Sunday!" *Southern Review,* 12 (Winter 1976), 156-157.

"Mary Flannery O'Connor." *The New Catholic Encyclopedia,* Vol. 10. New York: McGraw-Hill Book Co., 1967.

"Miss O'Connor Creates Unusual Humor Out of Original Sin." *Sewanee Review.* 71 (1963), 644-652.

"Notes on Ralph McGill: 1925-1929." An unpublished manuscript, Cheney Papers, Special Collections Department of the Jean and Alexander Heard Library of Vanderbilt University.

"Of the Old South, A Catharsis—A Personal Testimonial." *Telfair Enterprise,* n.d. Cheney Papers, Special Collections Department of the Jean and Alexander Heard Library of Vanderbilt University.

"Peter Taylor's Plays." *Sewanee Review,* 70 (Autumn 1962), 579-587.

"To Restore a Fragmented Image." *Sewanee Review,* 69 (Autumn 1961), 691-700.

Reviews:

"Bastard King in Exile." Rev. of *Ely*, by Ely Green. *Sewanee Review*, 76 (Winter 1968), 23-25.

"Is There a Voice Unheard in Warren's book *Who is Speaking for the Negro?*" *Sewanee Review*, 74 (Spring 1966), 545-550.

"*Lightwood*." Autobiographical sketch for the publication of the novel. *Atlanta Constitution*, 26 November 1939.

Rev. of *Katherine Anne Porter*: *A Critical Symposium*, ed. Lodwick Hartley and George Core. *Southern Humanities Review*, 4 (Fall 1970), 385-388.

"Secular Society as Deadly Farce." Rev. of *The Last Gentleman*, by Walker Percy. *Sewanee Review*, 75 (Spring 1967), 345-350.

"See Here, Private Cheney." Autobiographical sketch for the publication of *River Rogue*. *Atlanta Constitution*, 29 November 1942, p. 8.

"Stout Partisan Makes Attack on Liberalism." Rev. of *Up from Liberalism*, by William Buckley. *Nashville Banner*, n.d.

"Tenuous Moral Vision." Rev. of *The Middle of the Journey* and *Prothalamium*, by Philip Toynbee. *Sewanee Review*, 56 (Winter 1948), pp. 152-156.

"Too Late, Too Soon." Rev. of *Southern Politics*, by V. O. Key. *Sewanee Review*, 58 (Spring 1950), 374-378.

"Tremendous Tale of Epic Proportions." Rev. of *The Velvet Horn*, by Andre Lytle. *Nashville Banner*, 16 August 1957, p. 24.

"Uncle Sam's Other Province: Propaganda Novels about the South." *Sewanee Review*, 53 (Winter 1945), 147-152.

"What Endures in the South?" Rev. of *The Lasting South*, ed. James J. Kilpatrick and Louis Rubin, Jr. *Modern Age* (Fall 1958), pp. 408-410.

"Whither the Permanent Things in a Changing World?" Rev. of *Enemies of the Permanent Things*, by Russell Kirk. *Sewanee Review*, 78 (1970), 379-383.

Cited Correspondence:

Letters from Brainard Cheney:

Beatty, Dick. 3 June 1961.
Brooks, Paul. 20 February 1940.
Davis, Harold. 6 August 1949.
Jessup, Edwin. 5 September 1956.
Hartke, Father Gilbert V. 1955.
Koch, Vivienne. 24 August 1961.
Rider, Harry. 23 December 1942.
Stritch, Tommy. 8 April 1948.

Warren, Robert Penn. 9 November 1945, 6 May 1946,
and 9 August 1954.

Letters to Brainard Cheney:

Bess, George. 26 November 1958.

Brooks, Paul. 20 February 1940, May 1939, 28 September 1948.

Davidson, Donald. 28 May 1948, 10 July 1948.

Gordon, Caroline. 16 February 1952, 26 May 1939, 9
February 1937, 31 October 1939, 12 March
1937, Winter 1939, March 1932.

Joseph, Nannine. 10 March 1937.

Samples, David. 24 March 1957.

Tate, Allen. 30 August 1951.

Warren, Robert Penn. November 1945, 6 May 1946, 31
March 1960.

Others:

Fadiman, James. Letter to Nannine Joseph. 30 April
1942.

Interviews:

Personal Interviews with Brainard Cheney
in Smyrna, Tennessee with this author:

5 November 1976
12 December 1976

18 January 1977

25 January 1977

18 February 1977

11 April 1977

Others:

Cheney, Frances Neel. 23 February 1979 in Smyrna, Tennessee.

Tribune, 16 August 1942.

Part II. Works Cited

Chapter I: Early Life in Rural Georgia

Bess, George. "To Brainard Cheney." 26 Nov. 1958. *Brainard Cheney Papers*. Nashville, TN: Special Collections Department of the Jean and Alexander Heard Library of Vanderbilt University. Print.

Cheney, Brainard. Interview. Smyrna, TN. 5 Nov. 1976.

Cheney, Brainard. Interview. Smyrna, TN. 12 Dec. 1976.

Cheney, Brainard. "To Edwin Jessup." 5 Sept. 1956. *Brainard Cheney Papers*. Nashville, TN: Special Collections Department of the Jean and Alexander Heard Library of Vanderbilt University. Print.

"Of the Old South, A Catharsis—A Personal Testimonial." *Telfair Enterprise*. Print.

Chapter II: Student and Reporter

Cheney, Brainard. Interview. Smyrna, TN. 5 Nov. 1976.

Cheney, Brainard. Interview. Smyrna, TN. 12 Dec. 1976.

Cheney, Brainard. Interview. Smyrna, TN. 18 Jan. 1977.

Cheney, Brainard. Interview. Smyrna, TN. 25 Jan. 1977.

Cheney, Brainard. "To Harry Rider." 23 Dec. 1942. *Brainard Cheney Papers*. Nashville, TN: Special Collections Department of the Jean and Alexander Heard Library of Vanderbilt University. Print.

"Cheney Leaves Banner Staff: Recalls 15 years as Journalist." *Nashville Banner*. 2 April 1940: n. pag. Print.

"Cheney Leaving Banner to Write Another Novel." *Nashville Banner*. 2 April 1940: n. pag. Print.

Durant, Will. *Transitions*. New York: Garden City Publishing Company, 1927. Print.

Fugitives' Reunion: Conversations at Vanderbilt. R.R. Purdy ed. Nashville: Vanderbilt University Press. 1959, Print.

Martin, Harold H. *Ralph McGill, Reporter*. Boston: Little, Brown and Company. 1973. Print.

"Notes on Ralph McGill: 1925-1929." *Brainard Cheney Papers*. Nashville, TN: Special Collections Department of the Jean and Alexander Heard Library of Vanderbilt University. Print.

Chapter III: The Literary Influence of Caroline Gordon

Beatty, Richmond Croom et al. eds. *The Literature of the South*. Chicago: Scott, Foresman and Company, 1952. Print.

Bradbury, John M. *Renaissance in the South*. Chapel Hill: University of North Carolina Press, 1962. Print.

Cheney, Brainard. Interview. Smyrna, TN. 18 Feb. 1977.

Cheney, Brainard. "To Harold Davis." 6 Aug. 1949. *Brainard Cheney Papers*. Nashville, TN: Special Collections Department of the Jean and Alexander Heard Library of Vanderbilt University. Print.

Gordon, Caroline. *How to Read a Novel*. New York: Viking, 1957. Print.

Gordon, Caroline. "To Brainard Cheney." March 1932. *Brainard Cheney Papers*. Nashville, TN: Special Collections Department of the Jean and Alexander Heard Library of Vanderbilt University. Print.

Gordon, Caroline. "To Brainard Cheney." 9 Feb. 1937. *Brainard Cheney Papers*. Nashville, TN: Special Collections Department of the Jean and Alexander Heard Library of Vanderbilt University. Print.

Gordon, Caroline. "To Brainard Cheney." 12 March 1937. *Brainard Cheney Papers*. Nashville, TN: Special Collections Department of the Jean and Alexander Heard Library of Vanderbilt University. Print.

Gordon, Caroline. "To Brainard Cheney." Winter 1939. *Brainard Cheney Papers*. Nashville, TN: Special Collections Department of the Jean and Alexander Heard Library of Vanderbilt University. Print.

Gordon, Caroline. "To Brainard Cheney." 31 Oct. 1939. *Brainard Cheney Papers*. Nashville, TN: Special Collections Department of the Jean and Alexander Heard Library of Vanderbilt University. Print.

Gordon, Caroline and Allan Tate. *The House of Fiction*. New York: Scribner's, 1950. Print.

Ragan, David. "Portrait of a Lady Novelist: Caroline Gordon." *Mark Twain Quarterly* 7 (1947): 18. Print.

Squires, Radcliffe. *Allan Tate and His Work*. Minneapolis: University of Minneapolis Press. 1972. Print.

Thomson, John. "Putting Agrarianism into Practice." *The Tennessean*. 27 June 1937: 6. Print.

Chapter IV: *Lightwood*: A Novel of the Land Battles of Post-Civil War Georgia, 1870-1890

Brooks, Paul. "To Brainard Cheney." May 1939. *Brainard Cheney Papers*. Nashville, TN: Special Collections Department of the Jean and Alexander Heard Library of Vanderbilt University. Print.

Brooks, Paul. "To Brainard Cheney." 20 Feb. 1940. *Brainard Cheney Papers*. Nashville, TN: Special Collections Department of the Jean and Alexander Heard Library of Vanderbilt University. Print.

Cheney, Brainard. Interview. Smyrna, TN. 18 Feb. 1977.

Cheney, Brainard. *Lightwood*. Boston: Houghton Mifflin Company, 1939. Print.

Cheney, Brainard. "Lightwood (condensed)" *Scribner's Commentator*. N.d. n. pag. Print.

Cheney, Brainard. Rev. of *Lightwood*, by Brainard Cheney. *The Atlanta Constitution* 26 Nov. 1939: 9. Print.

Cheney, Brainard. *World Beyond Words.* TS *Brainard Cheney Papers.* Nashville, TN: Special Collections Department of the Jean and Alexander Heard Library of Vanderbilt University. Print.

Gordon, Caroline. "To Brainard Cheney." 9 Feb. 1937. *Brainard Cheney Papers.* Nashville, TN: Special Collections Department of the Jean and Alexander Heard Library of Vanderbilt University. Print.

Gold, W. J. Rev. of *Lightwood,* by Brainard Cheney. *Saturday Review of Literature* 28 Oct. 1939: 6. Print.

Gordon, Caroline. "To Brainard Cheney." 26 May 1939. *Brainard Cheney Papers.* Nashville, TN: Special Collections Department of the Jean and Alexander Heard Library of Vanderbilt University. Print.

Joseph, Nannine. "To Brainard Cheney." 10 March 1937. *Brainard Cheney Papers.* Nashville, TN: Special Collections Department of the Jean and Alexander Heard Library of Vanderbilt University. Print.

Rubin, Louis D. and Robert D. Jacobs eds. *Southern Renaissance.* Baltimore: The John Hopkins Press, 1953. Print.

The Tasters Cup. Cambridge: The Riverside Press, 1939. Print.

Time. 30 Oct. 1939: 71. Print.

Walton, E. H. Rev. of *Lightwood,* by Brainard Cheney. *New York Times* 5 Nov. 1939: 7 Print.

Chapter V: *River Rogue*: A Novel of the Rise and Fall of a

Timber Baron

"21-Day Voyage Retraces Course of Colonel Donelson." *Nashville Banner* 24 April. 1939: Front page. Print.

Adventure II, Manuscript of the River Voyage. N.d. TS. Cheney Papers.

Brooks, Paul. Letter to Brainard Cheney. 28 Sept. 1948.

Cheney, Brainard. Letter to Paul Brooks. 30 April 1942.

Cheney, Brainard. "Look-a, Look-a Yonder—I See Sunday!" *Southern Review.* 12 (1976): 156-157. Print.

Cheney, Brainard. Rev. of *River Rogue*, by Brainard Cheney. *Time* 10 Aug. 1942: 94. Print.

Cheney, Brainard. *River Rogue.* Boston: Houghton Mifflin, 1942. Print.

Cheney, Brainard. "See Here, Private Cheney." Rev. of *River Rogue*, by Brainard Cheney. *Atlanta Constitution* 29 Nov. 1942: 8. Print.

Cheney, Brainard. "Travel Deluxe: The Lumber Raft Way." *Atlanta Journal* 5 Dec. 1940: 14 Print.

"Cheney Ready to Start on River Trip." *Nashville Banner.* 3 April. 1939: Front page. Print.

Davidson, Donald. Rev. of *River Rogue*, by Brainard Cheney. *Sewanee Review* Jan. 1943: 165. Print.

"East Georgia Backcountry." *Saturday Review of Literature.* 25 Sept. 1942: 25. Print.

Fadiman, James. Letter to Joseph Nannine. 30 April 1942.

Faulkner, William. *Absalom! Absalom!* New York: The Modern Library, 1951. Print.

"Fire on Motor Boat Costs Life." *Tennessee Gazette* 8 April. 1939: n. pag. Print.

Chapter VI: The Battle for Washington

"Conservatism." *International Encyclopedia of the Social Sciences.* 1968.

Cheney, Brainard. *The Image and the Cry.* Unpublished novel, *Brainard Cheney Papers*. Nashville, TN: Special Collections Department of the Jean and Alexander Heard Library of Vanderbilt University. Print.

Cheney, Brainard. Interview. Smyrna, TN. 4 April 1977.

Cheney, Brainard. Interview. Smyrna, TN. 18 Feb. 1977

Cheney, Brainard. Telegraph to Senator Tom Stewart. 7 Dec. 1942. Brainard Cheney Papers, Joint University Library, Nashville, TN.

Cheney, Brainard. "To Robert Penn Warren." 9 Nov. 1945 *Brainard Cheney Papers*. Nashville, TN: Special Collections Department of the Jean and Alexander Heard Library of Vanderbilt University. Print.

Cheney, Brainard. "To Tom Stewart." 22 Nov. 1945. *Brainard Cheney Papers*. Nashville, TN: Special Collections Department of the Jean and Alexander Heard Library of Vanderbilt University. Print.

Davidson, Donald. "To Brainard Cheney." 10 July 1948. *Brainard Cheney Papers*. Nashville, TN: Special Collections Department of the Jean and Alexander Heard Library of Vanderbilt University. Print.

Gordon, Caroline. "To Brainard Cheney." 16 Feb. 1962. *Brainard Cheney Papers*. Nashville, TN: Special Collections Department of the Jean and Alexander Heard Library of Vanderbilt University. Print.

Squires, Radcliffe and Allen Tate. *A Literary Biography*. New York: Pegasus, 1971. Print.

Warren, Robert Penn. *All the King's Men*. New York: Harcourt, Brace, and World Inc., 1946. Print.

Warren, Robert Penn. "To Brainard Cheney." 9 November 1945 and 6 May 1946. *Brainard Cheney Papers*. Nashville, TN: Special Collections Department of the Jean and Alexander Heard Library of Vanderbilt University. Print.

Chapter VII: Religion, Politics, and Polemics

Cheney, Brainard. "Christianity and the Tragic Vision— Utopianism U.S.A." *Sewanee Review*. 69.4 (1961): 515-533. Print.

Cheney, Brainard. Interview. Smyrna, TN. 11 April 1977.

Cheney, Brainard. "Act I, Scene I." *Strangers in This World*. *Brainard Cheney Papers*. Nashville, TN: Special Collections Department of the Jean and Alexander Heard Library of Vanderbilt University. Print.

Cheney, Brainard. "The Leader Follows—Where?" *Georgia Review*. 2 (1948): 3-9. Print.

Cheney, Brainard. "To Father Gilbert V. Hartke." 1952. *Brainard Cheney Papers*. Nashville, TN: Special Collections Department of the Jean and Alexander Heard Library of Vanderbilt University. Print.

Cheney, Brainard. "To Robert Penn Warren." 9 Aug. 1954. *Brainard Cheney Papers*. Nashville, TN: Special Collections Department of the Jean and Alexander Heard Library of Vanderbilt University. Print.

Cheney, Brainard. "To Tommy Stritch." 8 April 1948. *Brainard Cheney Papers*. Nashville, TN: Special Collections Department of the Jean and Alexander Heard Library of Vanderbilt University. Print.

Cheney, Brainard. "To Dick Beatty." 3 June 1961. *Brainard Cheney Papers*. Nashville, TN: Special Collections Department of the Jean and Alexander Heard Library of Vanderbilt University. Print.

Cheney, Brainard. "What Endures in the South." *Modern Age*. 2 (1958): 409-410. Print.

Clement, Frank G. Lewiston, Idaho. 19 March 1954. Speech.

Clement, Frank G. Yakima, Washington. 20 March 1954. Address.

Cox, Marshall. "*Strangers in This World* Called Best VU Production." *Nashville Tennessean*. 17 Feb. 1952: n. pag. Print.

Davidson, Donald. "To Brainard Cheney." 28 May 1948. *Brainard Cheney Papers*. Nashville, TN: Special Collections Department of the Jean and Alexander Heard Library of Vanderbilt University. Print.

Dykeman, Wilma. "Too Much Talent in Tennessee?" *Harper's Magazine*. June. 1955: 49. Print.

Gordon, Caroline. "To Brainard Cheney." 16 Feb. 1962. *Brainard Cheney Papers*. Nashville, TN: Special Collections Department of the Jean and Alexander Heard Library of Vanderbilt University. Print.

Griggs, Alan, "The Rhetorical Rise and Fall of Tennessee Governor Frank G. Clement, 1952-1967" (1996). *Masters Theses & Specialist Projects*. Paper 799.

Obituary of Frank Clement. *New York Times*. 5 Nov. 1969: n. page. Print.

Samples, David. "To Brainard Cheney." 24 March 1957. *Brainard Cheney Papers*. Nashville, TN: Special Collections Department of the Jean and Alexander Heard Library of Vanderbilt University. Print.

Rader, Melvin and Bertram Jessup. *Art and Human Values*. Englewood Cliffs, New Jersey: Prentice-Hall, Inc., 1976. Print.

Ransom, John Crowe. "Poets without Laurels." *The Literature of the South*. Ed. Thomas Daniel Young et al. Glenview, Illinois: Scott, Foresman, and Company, 1968. Print.

"Religion and the Intellectuals." *Partisan Review*. N.d. 103-42, 215-56, 313-39, 456-83. Print.

Tate, Allen. "To Brainard Cheney." 30 Aug. 1951. *Brainard Cheney Papers*. Nashville, TN: Special Collections Department of the Jean and Alexander Heard Library of Vanderbilt University. Print.

Chapter VIII: *This is Adam*: A Novel of Grace and Duty in the Segregated South

Adams, John A. and Joan Martin Burke. *Civil Rights: A Current Guide to People, Organizations, and Events.* New York: R. R. Bowker Co., 1970. Print.

Britannica Book of the Year. Chicago: Encyclopedia Britannica Inc., 1958. Print.

Cheney, Brainard. "Has Teilhard de Chardin Really Joined the Within and the Without of Things?" *Sewanee Review.* 17 (1965): 217-236. Print.

Cheney, Brainard. "The Crocodile and the Crucifix: The Politics of Syncretism, Toynbeeism, and Revelation." *The Sewanee Review.* 66 (1958): 507-518. Print.

Cheney, Brainard. "Flannery O'Connor's Campaign for Her Country." *Sewanee Review.* 72 (1964): 555-558. Print.

Cheney, Brainard. "Caroline Gordon's 'Ontological Quest.'" *Renascence.* 16 (1963): 3-12. Print.

Cheney, Brainard. "Peter Taylor's Plays." *Sewanee Review.* 70 (1962): 579-587. Print.

Cheney, Brainard. *This Is Adam.* New York: McDowell, Obolensky, 1958. Print.

Cheney, Brainard. "To Robert Penn Warren." 27 June 1961. *Brainard Cheney Papers.* Nashville, TN: Special Collections Department of the Jean and Alexander Heard Library of Vanderbilt University. Print.

Cheney, Brainard. "To Vivian Koch." 24 Aug. 1961. *Brainard Cheney Papers.* Nashville, TN: Special Collections Department of the Jean and Alexander Heard Library of Vanderbilt University. Print.

Cheney, Brainard. *Quest of the Pelican*. N.d. TS. *Brainard Cheney Papers*. Nashville, TN: Special Collections Department of the Jean and Alexander Heard Library of Vanderbilt University. Print.

Lodge, David. "Novelist at the Crossroads." *The Novel Today*. Ed. Malcolm Bradbury. Totowa, New Jersey: Rowman and Littlefield, 1977. Print.

Marshal, John David. Rev. of *This Is Adam*. *Georgia Review*. 14 (1960): 117. Print.

McGill, Ralph. "*This Is Adam* Idea Came Thirty Years Ago." *Atlanta Constitution*. 14 Dec. 1958: n. pag. Print.

Purdy, R. R. "Profound Story Told with Consummate Skill." *Nashville Banner* 26 Sept. 1958: 25. Print.

Sullivan, Walter. "Local Author Writes Dramatic Third Novel." *Nashville Tennessean* 12 Sept. 1958: n. pag. Print.

Warren, Robert Penn. "To Brainard Cheney." 31 March 1960. *Brainard Cheney Papers*. Nashville, TN: Special Collections Department of the Jean and Alexander Heard Library of Vanderbilt University. Print.

Chapter IX: *Devil's Elbow*: A Novel of Redemption

Cheney, Brainard. *Devil's Elbow*. New York: Crown Publishers, Inc., 1969. Print.

W. W. Reader's Report. Crown Publishers, Inc. 4 April 1967. *Brainard Cheney Papers*. Nashville, TN: Special Collections Department of the Jean and Alexander Heard Library of Vanderbilt University. Print.

Chapter X: The Search for a Hero

Cheney, Brainard. *Devil's Elbow*. New York: Crown Publishers, Inc., 1968. Print.

Cheney, Brainard. *Lightwood*. Boston: Houghton Mifflin Company, 1939. Print.

Cheney, Brainard. "Look-a, Look-a Yonder—I See Sunday!" *Southern Review*. 12 (1976): 156-157. Print.

Cheney, Brainard. *River Rogue*. Boston: Houghton Mifflin Company, 1942. Print.

Cheney, Brainard. *This Is Adam*. New York: McDowell, Obolensky, 1958. Print.

Cheney, Brainard. "To Dick Beatty." 3 June 1961. *Brainard Cheney Papers*. Nashville, TN: Special Collections Department of the Jean and Alexander Heard Library of Vanderbilt University. Print.

Gordon, Caroline. "The Novels of Brainard Cheney." *Sewanee Review* 67 (1959): 330. Print.

Edinger, Edward. "Ego and Archetype. New York: G. P. Putnam's Sons, 1972.

Afterword:

Cheney, Francis Neel. Interview. Idler's Retreat, Smyrna, TN. 23 Feb. 1979.

Part III: Related Text

Andrews, M. P. (2013, Sept.). Brainard Cheney 1900-1990. *The New Georgia Encyclopedia*

Blotner, J. (1997). *Robert Penn Warren: A Biography*. New York, NY: Random House.

Beauchamp, Wilton Irving (1977). *Look a Yonder, I See Sunday: A Critical Study of the Novels of Brainard Cheney*. Atlanta, GA: Ph.D. diss., Emory University.

Gleaves, E. S. (1983). *Reference Services and Library Education: Essays in Honor of Frances Neel Cheney*. Lexington, MA.: D. C. Heath.

Marshall, J. D. (2001). "Remembering the Cheneys." *Tennessee Librarian , 52* (4).

Neel, R. (1993). Memories of Fannie. *Tennessee Librarian , 45*.

Stevens, R. C. (Ed.). (1986). *The Correspondence of Flannery O'Connor and the Brainard Cheneys*. Jackson, MS: University Press of Mississippi.

Underwood, T. A. (2003). *Allen Tate: Orphan of the South*. Princeton, NJ: Princeton University Press.

Waldron, A. (1987). *Close Connections: Caroline Gordon and the Southern Renaissance*. New York, Putnam.

Whigham, S. (Ed.). (2011). *The Lightwood Chronicles*. Eastman , GA: MM John Welda BookHouse.

Williams, Michael R. (2015). *Rivers, Rogues, & Timbermen in the Novels of Brainard Cheney*. Eastman, GA: MM John Welda BookHouse.

Williamson, J. *William Faulkner and Southern History*. New York, NY: Oxford Universtiy Press, Inc.

Zibart, G. (1976). "Fannie and Lon Cheney: Their Home is a Writers' Haven". *Vanderbilt Alumnus* (62), 20

Timeline for Brainard Cheney, 1900-1990

1900	Born on June 3, 1900, in Fitzgerald, Georgia, to Mattie Mood and Brainard Bartwell Cheney, Sr.
1906	Family moved from Fitzgerald to Lumber City, Georgia.
1908	Father died. Robin Bess, the overseer of the family's land holdings, became his male role model.
1916	Graduated from Lumber City High School, Georgia.
1917-19	Attended the Citadel in Charleston, South Carolina.
1918	Enlisted in the United States Army on November 12, as part of the Students Army Training Corps, and was Honorably Discharged on December 10.
1919-20	Bank Clerk in Lavonia, Georgia.
1920	Spent one semester at Vanderbilt University, Nashville, Tennessee.

McGill, Cheney joined the staff of the *Nashville Banner* newspaper as a police reporter. He continued with the *Banner* through 1942, serving as the City Hall, Courthouse, Federal and Capitol reporter; the city, wire, farm, financial, and aviation editor; and as a feature writer and editorial writer.

1927   Was in a terrible car wreck, as the result of driving heavily intoxicated. He was in the hospital for two months.

1928   Married Frances Neel Cheney June 21.

1931   Through their close friend, Robert Penn Warren, the Cheneys became acquainted with Allen Tate and Caroline Gordon, a friendship which had lasting importance to the Cheneys for religious reasons and to Brainard in particular for literary reasons.

1932   Manuscript for a novel, several short stories and poems burned in the Wesley Hall fire on the Vanderbilt campus.

1934-35   Worked on a novel titled *World Beyond Words*. Submitted for publication. Nannine Joseph, Caroline Gordon's literary agent, said he had great potential and suggested that he put this novel aside as experience and write a new one.

1936   Car wreck near Manchester, Tennessee. Cheney has minor injuries and another passenger was killed.

1937   Began work on a novel with the working title *The Squatter*, later published as *Lightwood*.

1939   Spent three weeks in April on the boat Adventure II, retracing the 1780 river voyage of Sam Donelson's Adventure from Fort Patrick Henry on the Holstein River to the banks of the Cumberland in Nashville, celebrating the historic establishment of Nashville. He submitted articles to the *Nashville Banner* each day of the trip.

1939   *Lightwood* published by Houghton Mifflin Company.

1940   Published *The Yellow Dress*, a short story, in the Contemporary Southern Prose anthology from D.C. Heath and Company. Began work on *River Rogue*, spent three months in Southern Georgia researching for the novel. Received a Fellowship to attend the Breadloaf Writers Conference in Vermont, where he met Wallace Stegner, Eudora Welty, Carson McCullers, and Robert Frost.

1941   Received a Guggenheim Fellowship to complete his second novel, *River Rogue*.

1942   *River Rogue* was published by Houghton Mifflin Company, and was (almost) chosen for the Book-of-the-Month Club. MGM held rights to make a movie but the project was deferred because of war.

1943-44   Served as Executive Secretary to Senator Tom Stewart of Tennessee. In 1943, the Tates had moved to Washington, D.C. when Allen Tate was appointed as the Library of Congress Poetry Chair. While living in Washington the Cheneys shared a home with the Tates and together they entertained many of their literary friends.

1944-45   Served as Secretary of Subcommittee on War Surplus Disposal of the Senate Small Business Committee.

1945-52   Wrote and rewrote a novel, *The Image and the Cry* five times. It was unpublished.

1949-50   Served as the Public Relations Director of the Greater Nashville Community Chest and wrote radio scripts and a movie script, entitled *Not Enough To Go Around*, on their behalf.

1950-51   Wrote the script for the play, *Strangers in This World*, the initial idea for this work came from a scene in *The Image and the Cry*. Received a Fellowship from the Huntington Hartford Foundation in Los Angeles.

1952   *Strangers in This World* was produced by the Vanderbilt University Theater, February 6-9. The Cheneys purchased land on St. Simon's Island off the coast of Southern Georgia. In August, he wrote a review of Flannery O'Connor's first novel, *Wise Blood*, which was to be the beginning of a very close friendship between the two writers.

1952-58   Served as Public Relations Director for Tennessee Governor Frank Clement.

1953   Became a member of the Roman Catholic Church. On June 6th Brainard and Frances met Flannery O'Connor for the first time, at her home outside Milledgeville, Georgia, on their way to St. Simon's Island.

1956-57   Through the auspices of the Tennessee Education and Dramatic Commission (1956) and the Sam Davis Outdoor Theater Project (1957) Cheney worked on a project to establish a State Theater and Workshop in Tennessee to produce plays by fiction writers.

1956   *Strangers in This World*, produced in Louisville, Kentucky at the Little Theater on the University of Louisville, Belknap Campus, January 26-28.

1958   *This Is Adam* published by McDowell Obolensky. Received a Literary Award from the Georgia Writers Association for the novel.

1959-60   Wrote *Quest of the Pelican*, offered for publication 1960-1964 and was then withdrawn.

1960   Another play, *I Choose to Die* was produced by Vanderbilt University Theatre, November 2-5.

1962   Cheney became very interested in the writings of the French Jesuit Priest, Pierre Teilhard de Chardin. Teilhard's book, *The Phenomenon of Man*, became paramount in Cheney's quest to reconcile science and religion.

1965   Co-Authored an essay on Teilhard de Chardin with Antonio Gotto titled, "Has Teilhard de Chardin Really Joined the Within and the Without of Things?", published in the *Sewanee Review*.

1969   His novel *Devil's Elbow* published by Crown Publishers.

1969-71   Worked on *In Pursuit of Happiness*. The novel was up for publication through Crown Publishers and had a release date but was never produced.

1970's   Worked on two novels, one titled *The People, The People*, and the other, a fictionalized history of his mother's family titled *Kitty Mood's Cup*.

1972   Sold the bulk of his papers to the Joint University Libraries, Vanderbilt University.

1981-82   Visited home town of Lumber City in April for Project RAFT, a celebration of the river culture and timber trade along the Ocmulgee, Oconee, and Altamaha rivers in Southern Georgia. Cheney was involved in the organization of Project RAFT with Dr. Delma Presley of Georgia Southern University. Cheney spoke at the Lumber City, Baxley, Jessup, and Darien town celebrations.

1982   Reprint of *River Rogue* with an Introduction by Robert Penn Warren was published by Burr Oak Publishers, Inc.

1984   Reprint of *Lightwood* with an Introduction by Delma E. Presley was published by Burr Oak Publishers, Inc. Cheney's nephew, Roy Neel, was instrumental in republishing both books with

Burr Oak.

1984   Terrye Newkirk submits *Cheers: Letters of Flannery O'Connor to Brainard and Frances Neel Cheney, 1953-1958* as Master's Thesis at Vanderbilt University.

1986   *The Correspondence of Flannery O'Connor and the Brainard Cheneys*, compiled by C. Ralph Stephens, is published by the University Press of Mississippi.

1990   Brainard Bartwell Cheney died on January 15, 1990 in Nashville, Tennessee, at the age of 89. Frances Neel Cheney died in 1996, also at the age of 89.

Index

About the Author

Dr. James Edwin Young II from Ferriday, Louisiana, received his BA in Philosophy and English at Tulane University and his Ph.D. from Peabody College of Vanderbilt University.

He teaches Southern Literature and Modern Intellectual Traditions at Weber State University and is the Director of the English Teaching Program. Dr. Young became acquainted with Brainard Cheney and his wife Francis Neel Cheney while working on his doctorate in the late 1970's.

His work has appeared in *Encyclia: The Journal of the Utah Academy of Sciences, Arts and Letters* and *The Journal of the International Society for Teacher Educators.*

This book is printed on acid free paper

Cover and design by Josh Sheffield

Additional assistance from Tom Hudson

www.ingramcontent.com/pod-product-compliance
Lightning Source LLC
Chambersburg PA
CBHW020452100426
42813CB00031B/3344/J